India's Macroeconomic Response to COVID-19

Karan Mehrishi

India's Macroeconomic Response to COVID-19

PETER LANG
Berlin · Bruxelles · Chennai · Lausanne · New York · Oxford

Bibliographic Information published by the Deutsche Nationalbibliothek
The Deutsche Nationalbibliothek lists this publication in the Deutsche Nationalbibliografie; detailed bibliographic data is available online at http://dnb.d-nb.de.

Library of Congress Cataloging-in-Publication Data
Library of Congress Control Number: 2025049345

ISBN 978-1-80374-715-6 (Print)
ISBN 978-1-80374-716-3 (E-PDF)
ISBN 978-1-80374-717-0 (E-PUB)
DOI 10.3726/b22279

Published by Peter Lang GmbH, Berlin (Germany)

info@peterlang.com - www.peterlang.com

This publication has been peer reviewed.

Dedicated to Mummy, Papa, and Guddu Chacha for bearing with my impossibilities

Contents

Figures

Tables

Foreword

The COVID-19 pandemic was an unprecedented global crisis, affecting every aspect of life across the world. The virus, first detected in Wuhan, China, quickly spread, bringing with it a dual threat: a massive public health emergency and an economic shockwave. As countries scrambled to protect their populations, economies came to a near standstill, forcing governments to respond with a range of economic interventions to prevent large-scale economic collapse.

India faced unique challenges in this situation. As a rapidly developing nation with a large and diverse population, the impact of the pandemic was profound not only in terms of lives lost but also in terms of economic disruption. The Indian government's response to the pandemic was complex and multifaceted, addressing both the fiscal and monetary needs of the nation in an effort to safeguard livelihoods and maintain economic stability. This book, *India's Macroeconomic Response to COVID-19*, provides an in-depth analysis of that response, documenting the measures taken, their outcomes, and the lessons learned for future generations.

The author, Karan Mehrishi, an economist with extensive experience in analysing India's financial systems, has made a commendable effort in chronicling the country's response to one of the most significant economic disruptions in recent history. Through this book, Mehrishi not only captures the fiscal and monetary interventions but also provides a broader understanding of the underlying mechanisms that shaped India's approach.

One of the most striking elements of India's response was the speed and scale of its fiscal and monetary interventions. With a gargantuan stimulus package estimated to be worth ₹45.06 lakh crore, the government acted quickly to safeguard financial institutions, stabilize markets, and provide relief to vulnerable sectors of the economy. The Reserve Bank of India (RBI) played a crucial role in ensuring liquidity, reducing interest rates, and creating mechanisms to protect both large corporations and smaller enterprises, such as Micro, Small, and Medium Enterprises (MSMEs), from insolvency. By lowering the repo rate by 115 basis points and aiding in interest subvention schemes, the RBI helped maintain the flow of credit in the economy, despite the severe disruptions caused by the lockdowns.

Lockdowns, though necessary to prevent the spread of the virus, resulted in massive economic losses. India's unorganized economy, which employs a significant portion of its population, was particularly hard-hit. Businesses were forced to close, workers lost their livelihoods, and capacity utilization in the manufacturing sector reached historic lows. In this environment, the Indian government's decision to prioritize saving lives, despite the economic fallout, was both courageous and necessary. As Mehrishi notes, the blanket ban on economic activity, while painful in the short term, helped prevent an even greater humanitarian disaster.

The structure of this book allows readers to gain a holistic understanding of the macroeconomic response, with each chapter carefully dissecting the various aspects of the fiscal and monetary packages introduced during the pandemic. Mehrishi explores the fiscal muscle flexed by the government to protect vulnerable sectors of the economy and the monetary accommodation provided by the RBI to ensure financial stability. He also delves into the results of the combined macroeconomic response, offering insights into how fiscal and monetary policies interacted during this critical period. The book's analysis of the Investment-Savings (IS) and Liquidity Management (LM) curves, and their limitations in explaining the response, adds a valuable theoretical dimension to the practical measures discussed.

One of the key takeaways from this work is the importance of coordination between fiscal and monetary policies during a crisis. As the author points out, India's response was not simply a series of isolated actions but a well-coordinated effort that involved multiple arms of the government and financial institutions working together to mitigate the effects of the pandemic. The simultaneous implementation of fiscal and monetary measures helped stabilize the economy, protect jobs, and ensure that businesses could continue operating, albeit under challenging conditions.

Mehrishi's work also provides a global context for India's response by comparing it with other countries' fiscal and monetary interventions. The pandemic was a global event, and liquidity creation in developed economies had a profound impact on capital markets worldwide. Understanding how India navigated this interconnected financial system, while maintaining its own macroeconomic stability, offers valuable lessons for policymakers not just in India but across the world.

In addition to documenting the successes, the author does not shy away from highlighting the challenges and shortcomings of the response. The speed and scale of the pandemic meant that decisions had to be made quickly, often with incomplete information. There were hits and misses, as is to be expected in a crisis of this magnitude. Yet, what stands out in this analysis is the resilience of the Indian economy and its ability to adapt to rapidly changing circumstances. The lessons derived from India's economic management during the pandemic will undoubtedly inform future policy-making, particularly in the areas of crisis response and economic resilience.

As the book moves towards its conclusion, it offers recommendations for future economic management based on the experiences of the COVID-19 pandemic. The author calls for greater preparedness, stronger safety nets for vulnerable populations, and more robust fiscal and monetary tools to manage future crises. These recommendations are particularly timely as the world continues to grapple with the long-term effects of the pandemic and considers how to build more resilient economies for the future.

Karan Mehrishi's *India's Macroeconomic Response to COVID-19* is not just a record of what transpired during the pandemic but also a critical analysis of the policies that helped India navigate one of the most challenging periods in its modern history. The book is an invaluable resource for economists, policymakers, and future generations seeking to understand the complexities of managing an economy during a global crisis. It stands as a testament to the diligence, planning, and hard work that went into protecting India's economy and its people during this unprecedented time.

Dr. Sandeep Ananthanarayanan

Acknowledgements

The author would like to thank Prof. A.K. Sengupta, eminent economist and former dean of the Indian Institute of Foreign Trade (IIFT), Delhi, for the honour he has bestowed on the book project as a reviewer.

CHAPTER 1

Introduction

India's macroeconomic response to the COVID-19 pandemic was a one-of-a-kind exercise involving a $3 trillion + economy.[1] It was a seamless transition of a growth-oriented economic policy into one that is sustaining. India's combined fiscal and monetary response is estimated to be valued at ₹45.06 lac crore.[2]

The purpose of the work is to assess this macroeconomic response and record the details of both the monetary and fiscal packages created to fight the pandemic. The author believes that chronicling India's macroeconomic response will be a great service to future generations, who would like to refer to the great planning, diligence, and hard work that were involved in protecting India from not only an economic catastrophe but also an unprecedented humanitarian disaster.

Book Project Background

COVID-19 pandemic was reported to have been caused by a virus that had originated in the city of Wuhan, capital of the south-eastern province of Hubei in China. While initially, the spread of this virus was localized, with minimal contagion in the rest of the Chinese mainland, international travellers rapidly proliferated infections to the rest of the world.

1 Macrotrends: India GDP 1960–2022 | https://www.macrotrends.net/countries/IND/india/gdp-gross-domestic-product#:~:text=India%20gdp%20for%202021%20was,a%201.94%25%20increase%20from%202017.

2 Author's estimate based on Government of India Data | Atmanirbhar Package Report

A few cases began to appear in India in early 2020. By March 2020, however, the case load factor increased substantially, ensuing in a complete 21-day lockdown. This was, however, just a start as multiple lockdowns in varied intensities were enforced in India, taking a significant toll on economic activity. The idea behind the lockdown was to save lives, irrespective of the economic loss this would cause. The lockdown was kind of a blanket ban on almost all economic activity, except certain essential services.

As a result, manufacturing capacities were permanently impaired, and capacity utilization levels were at an all-time low. To protect the Indian economy from collapse, the government's initial response was to safeguard the financial institutions. Once these institutions were secured via adequate liquidity (infused by the RBI), the next step was to take care of vulnerable corporations, which were facing heightened credit risk on the back of negative cash flows. While preserving jobs, the government's initial fiscal response was to provide support to employee sustenance programmes and interest subvention schemes.

The Reserve Bank of India (RBI), in turn, reduced interest rates by 115 bps,[3] first via an out-of-turn monetary policy committee (MPC) meeting and then gradually bringing the Repo rate to 4 per cent and the Reverse Repo to 3.35 per cent by May 2020. The RBI also introduced several schemes for the benefit of Non-Banking Financial Companies (NBFCs) as well as MSMEs. Also, the identification process of Non-Performing Assets (NPAs) and Special Mention Accounts (SMAs) was effectively slowed, and restructuring exercises were encouraged amidst accommodative monetary policy.

Eventually, the ensuing lockdown led to the loss of 5,30,690[4] Indian lives and amounted to an economic loss that cannot be estimated, given India's largely unorganized economy. The project, therefore, pertains to a detailed assessment of India's macroeconomic response to the COVID-19 pandemic from both the fiscal as well as monetary perspectives. Since the response not only included the flexing of the fiscal muscle but also monetary

3 RBI Monetary Policy Meeting Summary | https://www.rbi.org.in/Scripts/BS_PressReleaseDisplay.aspx?prid=49700

4 Google Covid Death Toll Statistics (India Page) | https://news.google.com/covid19/map?hl=en-IN&mid=%2Fm%2F03rk0&gl=IN&ceid=IN%3Aen

accommodation, the project's review includes both the Ministry of Finance as well as the RBI.

The project is divided into twelve chapters, including this introduction. The second chapter pertains to the run-up to COVID-19 and talks about the macroeconomic situation of India at the time the pandemic hit. The third chapter describes the 'Fiscal Response to the Covid-19' pandemic, and this is followed by the fourth chapter on India's 'Monetary Response'.

These three chapters include details about the pre-pandemic landscape and the post-event fiscal and monetary packages introduced by the government of India to support the economy. Also, there will be details about the net and gross debt mobilization during the time. Since it is understood that the individual fiscal and monetary responses were successful in managing the economy as a combination, the fifth chapter pertains to 'Results of the Combined Macroeconomic Response'.

The idea behind this chapter is that in macroeconomic terms, fiscal response is followed by an equivalent monetary response and therefore lessons can be drawn from the interactions between the IS and the LM curves. Although the Hicks–Hanson Model does not seem to adequately explain this operation, as interest rates were lowered when fiscal muscle was being flexed. Nevertheless, no analysis can be complete without studying the simultaneous influences of fiscal and monetary sides on each other.

The chapter also concerns itself with the learnings derived as lessons from the pandemic-related emergency, economic management. It must be noted that an event of this magnitude has occurred after 100-odd years, and the global system was not prepared to deal with it effectively, given its interconnectedness.

The response, therefore, provides several lessons for the public as well as policymakers alike. Also, rapid vaccine development, as well as financial support to pharmaceutical companies, had its own share of complications. Nonetheless, managing the economy during such a tumultuous period had certain hits and misses, which need to be documented.

The sixth chapter is an assessment of the global response to COVID-19, and how it impacted India. The idea here is to provide a round-up of the monetary and fiscal response elsewhere in the world, as rapid liquidity creation flooded the global system, raising all boats. Capital market characteristics, therefore, hold the key to our understanding.

Since the author believes that the assessment of global central bank balance sheets is essential to understand the true impact of fiscal-monetary coordination, the seventh chapter provides a deep dive into monetary management. The chapter includes a detailed understanding of the evolution of major central bank (US Federal Reserve, ECB, Bank of Japan) balance sheets, in conjunction with liquidity provisions, and fiscal responses.

The eighth chapter consists of the 'Recommendations & Learnings' that are derived from the lessons learnt from the economic management experiments during the pandemic. This is, however, preceded by policy recommendations that could have strengthened India's monetary response to COVID-19 (for that matter, any crisis response) had they been adopted earlier. There are important discussions on r*, a modified policy framework focusing on liquidity targeting and system collateral diversity.

The following ninth chapter includes a discussion on the mathematical models utilized for forecasting during the pandemic. This is an important discussion because this was a black-swan event, and traditional models did not provide a meaningful understanding of the evolving macros.

Significant work was therefore done by the ECB, as well as Federal Reserve economists, to build models using engineering physics techniques for the prediction of data in real time. Ultimately, the discussed models contributed a great deal to predicting the real impact of the pandemic on both macro as well as micro levels, and helped anticipate the level of fiscal stimulus/monetary accommodations necessary in real time.

This author also believes that COVID-19 was more of a human tragedy than just being considered an economic crisis. Therefore, it becomes all the more important to add a chapter on the experiences of real people working in public service on the management of the COVID-19 pandemic on the ground level. This chapter includes perspectives from people of four different countries to add diversity to the thoughts of the author, who is Indian by citizenship. A kaleidoscope of human emotions adds depth to this project, justifying its existence as a work on one of history's most significant health crises.

Finally, the work ends with the eleventh and twelfth chapters: 'Conclusion', and 'Literature Review.' This section comprises the gist of the author's research and includes a way forward, followed by a detailed description of some of the most interesting work covering the macro responses on pandemic management by other authors and economists.

CHAPTER 2

A Run-up to COVID-19 Economy: India's Evolving Macroeconomic Landscape in the COVID Year 2020

David Hume, the renowned Scottish philosopher, had a very interesting way of describing a Black Swan Event. "No amount, of observations of white swans can allow the inference that all swans are white, but the observation of a single black swan is sufficient to refute that conclusion," he once said. The COVID-19 pandemic and its impact on the Indian economy is perhaps one instance when such inference can be drawn, or rather refuted. No amount of empirical research could have given the answers that we sought, at the start of the pandemic, not on economics, not on society, and definitely not on the future.

The last week of May 2020 was eventful, especially because it gave us a glimmer of how our collective output actually fared. Even though the GDP number pertained to a year gone by, it definitely acted as a precedent of what to expect in the current financial year. This was especially important because 2020 was facing the above-described Black Swan event that nobody anticipated before.

The previous year, i.e., 2019, was, however, not impacted much by this event, and its performance showed us what the actual state of the economy really was, to start with. According to this author's understanding, as a monetary economist, the potential growth of the Indian economy for the Financial Year 2020 was in the range of 5.5–6 per cent. This assumes that all things being equal, the nation's economy would have grown by at least this much, considering its past performances.

The world is, however, not perfect, and accordingly, potential is rarely reached, and therefore, we witnessed actual real growth of 4.2 per cent, as per the estimates of the Ministry of Statistics (MOSPI). What this means is that the Indian economy, at the time, faced an output gap, equivalent to ~1.8 per cent of real GDP, due to factors unknown or, in most cases, figured out via guesswork.

Analysing the official numbers from both the demand and supply sides of the argument, we can find a great deal of uniformity. This is, in turn, connected to the relationship between the fiscal muscle and household appetite.

Speaking generally, both these variables play a critical role in the demand and supply side of things by virtue of being the drivers of the economic virtuous cycle. Consequently, we note that whichever way one looks at it, the fiscal muscle reigned supreme, while the households played the second fiddle.

From the aggregate demand perspective, final Government expenditure was perhaps the only variable growing in double digits – 11.8 per cent. Meanwhile, household final consumption expenditure grew by a comparatively low (positively, nonetheless) 5.3 per cent. Furthermore, extending the aggregate supply side argument, the central Government's total revenue was short by ₹9.5 lac crore for that year, with tax revenue down by nearly ₹1.5 lac crore. This resulted in the fiscal deficit reaching 4.6 per cent from 3.8 per cent, which was earlier estimated.

Lower tax revenue also means that the household appetite was considerably lower than expected because they ended up spending less money on consumption. The economy too recorded a growth of almost 3 per cent less, a factor that sums up the actual versus potential argument. Importantly, the potential growth was just lower by 180 bps, so what explained the additional 120 bps output loss? Was it another unprecedented Black Swan event? The debate raged on.

Given the fact that capacity utilization levels had remained below the critical 70 per cent mark for quite some time, previously, it was only a matter of time before we would have begun to see the output gap widen. The reasons here could have been anyone's guess – systemic inefficiencies, lack of financing avenues, lack of strategic planning and or simply, ineffective democracy? Now that India has grown below its potential, what happens to the money that was generated anyway by way of the fiscal expansion along with the foreign money inflows?

Consider the following argument:

$$\text{No consumption} = \text{savings?}$$

Possibly.

A lot of this money went to the banks, which used it to expand the fiscal muscle even further by purchasing even more Government securities rather than just lending it out. Some of it went into currency in circulation (CIC), while another portion again went to the banks via deposits, which maintained a healthy, consistent growth of over 9.5 per cent. The quantum left behind became inflationary due to the lack of productive use. And that became not just a barnacle, but a tough nut to crack for the policymakers.

But then this was collateral damage in the mandate to ensure a larger good. Examining non-productive use of money, a contraction in capital formation (−2.8 per cent) is very unhealthy for a developing country such as India, which needs to create and maintain employment for its over 450 million, and growing labour force.

Amongst sectorial performances, while some labour-absorbing core sectors were pulled up by fiscal accommodation, most others recorded contractions on the back of slowing household consumption. Agriculture remained a lone wolf, non-core sector that managed a comparatively competitive 4 per cent, but in any case, this author believes that the sector's potential to generate sufficient jobs or value added remains questionable, to say the least.

Despite agriculture's surprising performance on the back of a healthy monsoon in the previous year, food articles (Wholesale Price Index, WPI) apparently inflated by 8.4 per cent. In terms of CPI too, food articles inflated by over 6.8 per cent in April alone. Given the weight of the food basket in the consumer inflation index, it is not difficult to understand the situation that the economy was finding itself in.

CMIE's unemployment index, which at the time claimed that unemployment was still over 25 per cent, was pointing to a very grim future that awaited both policymakers and actual people on the ground. Black Swan? Perhaps not. Notwithstanding, combined with the year 2020's economic performance due to the COVID crisis, things were expected to get even worse, and they did!

In the first week of June 2020, the RBI released the minutes of the meeting of the 23rd MPC that was held between May 20th and 22nd 2020. The statement included deliberations of the time's six members, who also happen to be a few of the nation's top economists. The committee had elected to cut the policy rate (repo) by 40 bps to 4 per cent during this meeting. No surprises were in store when it came to the Reverse Repo, which figuratively was the lowest hurdle rate in monetary policy at the time (before it was effectively replaced by the Standing Deposit Facility (SDF).

The Reverse Repo Rate went down by a comparable 40 bps to 3.35 per cent. All committee members were unanimous in their decision to cut rates and cited similar arguments except external member Chetan Ghate, who instead recommended a rate cut of 25 bps. While all other members were of the view that further stimulus was necessary by way of further rate cuts, given the irreversible damage caused by the COVID-19 crises, Ghate believed that it was too early to exhaust most monetary ammunition.

He stated that the committee must leave some "dry powder" for the time when it is actually needed. What he meant by his "dry powder" argument was that the economy was still in stasis and could require stimulus when the demand side was fully activated. What struck me, however, was his concern regarding the so-called demand-supply mismatch, which opens a totally different plane of thinking. According to him, the economy will most definitely face a situation where the demand side will outcompete the supply side, as and when the lockdown is lifted completely.

It was argued that in such a situation, the MPC most likely would have two options:

1. It could remain accommodative – further aiding the incoming pent-up demand.

   or

2. Take stock of the evolving picture early on.

The second condition, in all senses and purposes, seemed realistic and, importantly, logical, given the domestic and international supply-side disruptions caused by the pandemic. But then, there really is no 'on/off' switch here that would have made the supply side come online at a moment's notice. For this reason, the MPC likely allowed the accommodation to last longer than required. Amidst uncertainty, in a way, this strategy cannot be faulted either. Eventually, the country did come to terms with the massive migrant exodus, which resulted in insufficient availability of man-power across the economy.

Low-capacity utilization levels and sceptical banks further abstained the industry players from firing on all cylinders in preparation for the demand finally coming back with full force. In other words, it can be argued that the industry wasn't prepared to absorb the tsunami that was expected to be brought about by the much-touted V-shaped recovery.

Inflation was the next logical offshoot of such an anomaly. And it soon turned out to be true. It may be argued that the April 2020 CPI number (just as the month before it) left much to be desired due to its limited scope. The metric has been largely based on food inflation, which was sticky.

Widely known already, food inflation was showing considerable pressures since the beginning of the previous financial year's third quarter (Q3 FY20) and showed little signs of abating. Along with the MPC members, however, most economists at the time believed that the effects of food inflation were transitionary at best, as the Rabi Season was expected to be healthy. Not to mention the impact of rising crude prices was ignored, since the fact remains that low prices never really translated into benefits for Indian consumers in the first place.

The concern that should have attracted more attention at the time pertained to core inflation, which was strangely left out of active analyst considerations. During the lockdown, spending was primarily characterized by essentials rather than discretionary, and perhaps the timing of the transition could not be ascertained at the time.

It was therefore hoped that non-food inflation would remain under control, allowing the policy space to remain open, as pointed out by most MPC members during the May meeting. As per the expectations, if that assessment did not hold true, then supply disruptions would have most certainly led to inflationary tendencies and forced the committee to reconsider its accommodative stance in the medium term. The excess systemic liquidity, which eventually did not translate into meaningful economic activity, was another threat that policymakers missed at the time.

Giving due cognizance to the evolving dynamic of low and, importantly, controlled inflation, as well as the high unemployment metric, the Indian economy was showing classic signs of what the short-run Phillips curve represents. The assumption states that in the short term, the relationship between inflation and unemployment remains inverse. In other words, in a country's economic environment – high unemployment and low inflation can co-exist. Worryingly, however, this negative correlation ceases in the longer term as repeated monetary and fiscal efforts lead to a rise in inflation while keeping high unemployment conditions intact.

This basically happens because of two primary reasons. Firstly, as the government tries to spend its way out of a slowdown (such as the COVID crisis), it raises more debt. Consequently, the RBI must print more money – increasing the CIC in the process. Following closely, even though not apparent at the time, given the accommodative stance, interest rates must invariably rise to control the resultant inflationary tendencies, eventually exhibited by the economy. This stifles the very capex that fiscal expansion intended to start by making both capital and labour expensive.

Unemployment, as a result, no longer influences inflation and resultantly rises simultaneously along with inflation. This is an inevitable part of the business cycle, but almost always forgotten by market participants, making hay while the accommodation lasted. None of the policymakers and market participants seriously considered the inevitable occurrence of such a condition post the crises. A policy oversight, the effects of which are visible only now.

Nevertheless, Indians prepared themselves for a rough ride early on, and higher prices were just one of the household considerations. As per RBI's forward-looking surveys, at the time, most interestingly, the Consumer Confidence Survey, over 79 per cent of the respondents believed that the price level would rise, and interestingly, the same was the case with inflation expectations.

Almost the same proportion expected prices/inflation to rise and remain high over a one-year horizon. In fact, as per the Household Inflation Expectations survey (IESH), respondents' expectation of median inflation rose by 190 bps in a 3-month horizon and 120 bps in a 12-month horizon as compared to the previous year. What was troubling was the fact that, based on those forward survey results, while most respondents believed that their spending would rise as a result of higher prices/ inflation, they overwhelmingly expected the economic climate and their employment status to diminish.

This leads us to the chicken and egg story, stating, 'If inflation horizon is expected to be under control and there is a policy space available, then economy will attain its potential sooner than later'. But for that to happen, people must keep their jobs (signs of a healthy supply side). However, since Indians were not expecting to keep their jobs and were sceptical about the economic climate, the output gap should have expanded further, leading to tons of 'created' money lying with the banks and public.

Inflation was therefore beginning to grow its tentacles deeper than previously anticipated. Amidst this action, being witnessed at the Mint Street, a bigger game was being played in Washington, DC, that no economist, worth his/her salt, could ignore. The Federal Reserve Open Market Committee (FOMC), through its 10th of June Minutes of Meeting, provided the state of the US Dollar and a glimpse of the evolving global liquidity. For starters, the 5th FOMC for calendar year 2020 kept the status quo and started with the US version of 'Whatever it, takes' argument by stating, 'The Federal Reserve is committed to using its full range of tools to support the US economy in this challenging time, thereby promoting its maximum employment and price stability goals'.

The committee maintained the interest rate at 10 bps and the Federal Funds Target Range of 0–25 bps. While the former is the equivalent of the Indian weighted average call money rate (WACR), the latter is the Indian equivalent of the policy corridor, which comprises Reverse Repo and the Marginal Standing Facility (MSF). These hurdle rates were one of the lowest seen in recent history and were last achieved during the 2008 financial crisis.

In order to accomplish the pre-ordained target range via the infusion of requisite liquidity, the FOMC had continued with its plan to increase the System Open Market Account holdings of Mortgage-Backed Securities, Commercial Mortgage-Backed Securities, and US Government Securities.

The transactions, as authorized were to be conducted via the Open Market Desk of the Federal Reserve's New York branch. Given these operations under what came to be known as Quantitative Easing 4 (QE4), the Federal Reserve expanded its balance sheet by over $2 trillion, compared to September 2019 and increased its purchases of the above-mentioned securities to $60 billion a week.

The drastic measures undertaken and ultimately hastened in the wake of the COVID-19 crisis had taken the balance sheet size to $7.22 trillion or 29 per cent of US GDP. What this means is that over $2 trillion of additional liquidity was created and circulated in the global system, searching for yields. Most certainly, a portion of this cheap money ended up in emerging markets such as India, helping market valuations to soar.

Back home, the RBI saw its balance sheet surge to an all-time high of over $600 billion. The number may sound peanuts as compared to its American counterpart, but it must be noted that this number represented almost 20 per cent of India's GDP and had the potential to cover 15 months' worth of imports at the time. This was significant given the fact that the Indian economy hardly created any additional value in the financial year, and the strong forex would supplement the Government's efforts in safeguarding national interests against any eventuality.

There are many explanations regarding this feat of the RBI, including the record-breaking FPI inflows into a subsidiary of a large Indian blue-chip company. However, what has been sorely missed by analysts is the role played by the revaluation gains experienced by foreign asset holdings, given the FOMC's continued purchases to the tune of $60 billion per week.

For all intents and purposes, the low prevalent interest rates abroad, which included the United States, European Union, and Japan, had resulted in yields falling massively, extensively increasing the valuations of the Foreign Sovereign Debt securities held by the RBI. Case in point is the RBI's holdings of American sovereign debt to the tune of $157 billion, most probably purchased at a yield of over 2 per cent.

Since the prevailing rates fell below 0.7 per cent, the valuations would have gone up notably. The situation was giving an extra boost to the already high forex reserves, which were riding on a solid US Dollar valuation (due to the crises-related volatility). In other news, to say that the domestic economy is underperforming was an understatement. While the liquidity situation seemed healthy, the co-existence of a lack of household demand for non-essential items and poor capacity utilizations levels resulted in a new normal of sub-optimal economic performance.

The situation's tendency to be inflationary is a topic already discussed, but the supply chain disruption of necessary items such as food commodities was definitely apparent over the months of April and May 2020. While the MOSPI did not reveal the full range of inflation numbers, which includes the overall May CPI number, it did provide a glimpse of the food consumer price index, which rose to 9.28 per cent. This was, of course, on the higher side compared to the trends witnessed in the recent past. Industrial production (IIP), as apparent from the above explanation, had been suffering since the lockdown began and reached an even lower level than was seen in the last quarter of the previous financial year. Such had been the impact that it was expected that the IIP would not even be influenced by the concept of 'favourable base effect' during the first half of 2020. As expected, the IIP for April contracted by 55 per cent on a YoY basis. Meanwhile, manufacturing sectors had contracted by almost 65 per cent during the same month. It was also noted that during that month, nationwide lockdowns were imposed to curb the spread of COVID-19 virus. Consequently, industrial activities, except for essential commodities such as food and medicine, were on a standstill.

The only sectors that recorded below 30 per cent contraction include food, petroleum, and pharmaceutical products. This, in a way, provided some kind of a safety net to industrials and helped restrict the IIP's fall beyond (−) 55 per cent.

Since the aforementioned sectors contribute to a higher share in overall IIP (more than 22 per cent), the economy's spirits sustained, amidst uncertainty. The dynamics of the global economy, therefore, continued to be influenced by respective central bank liquidity operations only. Since the monetary side is always capable of keeping things afloat and bringing about a sense of normalcy during difficult phases, the validity of the argument generally holds true. For rationalists among us, all eyes were on the speed at which household consumption would normalize, followed by a positive business sentiment. But until that time, however, supply chains of essential items were prioritized, strengthened, and streamlined, and policy actions were merely trial and error.

CHAPTER 3

India's Fiscal Response to COVID-19

Policy Question: Was the Fiscal Response Sufficient?

The Government of India's fiscal response was immediate as it announced a package of ₹1.7 lac crore.[5] However, this package was primarily to finance the loss of tax revenue envisaged by the exchequer due to loss of tax revenue – resulting from lockdowns. Eventually, the government of India introduced a package worth 15 per cent of GDP or roughly ₹29.87 lac crore[6] until November 2020 (according to information available on PIB). Out of this quantum, 9 per cent of GDP came directly as government support, while the rest comes as accommodation from the RBI. By June FY21–22, the government announced the Atmanirbhar Bharat Package 4.0, worth ₹6.29 lac crore.[7] This took the total stimulus to around ₹36 lac crore.[8] Through parliamentary approval, the government of India was getting ready to borrow a net additional ₹4.2 lac crore,[9] which was part of the 5th tranche of the Atmanirbhar stimulus packages. When introduced, the total quantum of all stimulus packages released

5 Ministry of Finance | Press Bureau | Government of India | https://pib.gov.in/PressReleaseIframePage.aspx?PRID=1608345

6 Press Bureau | Government of India | Atmanirbhar Bharat Package Announcement | https://static.pib.gov.in/WriteReadData/userfiles/Atmanirbhar%20Package%203.0%20final%20final%20%20-%20Copy%201.pdf

7 Cabinet Approves Covid Stimulus Package for ₹6.29 lac crores | The Economic Times | https://economictimes.indiatimes.com/news/economy/policy/cabinet-approves-rs-6-29-lakh-crore-covid-19-relief-package-announced-by-fm/articleshow/83985109.cms?from=mdr

8 Authors Estimates Based on Government of India Data

9 Government Seeks Parliamentary Approval | Parliament Nod Sought for Extra Spend of ₹3.25 lac crores on Subsidy and Capex | https://economictimes.indiatimes.com/news/economy/finance/govt-seeks-parliament-nod-for-net-additional-spending-of-rs-3-25-lakh-cr-this-fiscal/articleshow/96106019.cms

until the end of FY23 (Fiscal + Monetary) is estimated to be around ₹45.06 lac crore. It must be noted that these packages are financed by the general tax revenue, cesses, along deficit financing. Therefore, the quantum earmarked, spawned from the fiscal side, is reflected in the budget mathematics (discussed at a later stage in this chapter). The following tables show Packages (Phase Wise) and the quantum of support available to intended recipients:

Table 1: Atmanirbhar Bharat Abhiyan 1.0 (Government's COVID-19 Package Highlights)[10] (Q1 FY20–21). Data sourced from Press Bureau (PIB), Government of India.

Recipient	Scheme	Quantum of Government Support
Street Vendors	PM SVANidhi Support	₹1,373.33 crore
Farmer Loans	Via the Kisan Credit Card Scheme	₹1,43,262 crore
Fisherfolk	Matsya Sampada Yojana	₹1,632.32 core
Farmer Loans (Working Capital)	Working Capital Loans (CC) via NABARD	₹25,000 crore
Corporate Borrowers	Emergency Credit Line Guarantee Scheme (ECLGS) 1.0	Sanctioned: ₹2,05,000 crore
Corporate Borrowers	Partial Credit Guarantee Scheme 2.0	₹26,889 crore
NBFCs	Special Liquidity Scheme	₹7,227 crore
Electricity Distribution Companies (DISCOMs)	DISCOMs Liquidity Injection Operation	₹1,18, 273 crore

The Atmanirbhar 1.0 Stimulus Package focused on the most vulnerable segments of the Indian economy. The government early on identified that farmers and agriculturally employed individuals will be most impacted given the lockdown-induced breakdown of logistics and financial accessibility.

In order to solve these problems faced by farmers/agriculturalists, the government of India introduced the ₹1.43 lac crore Kisan Credit Card Scheme, which was intended to help farmers access inputs without delay. The intention was that farmers are ready for the Kharif Season sowing, which generally starts sometime in June (Monsoon Season). Farmers were also provided with working

10 Press Bureau | Government of India | Atmanirbhar Bharat Package Announcement | https://static.pib.gov.in/WriteReadData/userfiles/Atmanirbhar%20Package%203.0%20final%20final%20%20-%20Copy%201.pdf

capital loans in association with NABARD worth ₹25,000 crore. These loans were to be used by farmers along with Kisan Credit Cards. The next target group were fisherfolk and street vendors, who were vulnerable because of a lack of access to their livelihoods, given the lockdown and embargo on daily consumers. Roughly ₹3000 crore were earmarked for the combined groups in order to support them in the difficult times.

To provide an uninterrupted power supply to households and critical service providers, the government decided to provide liquidity support to debt-ridden power distribution companies. The purpose of the exercise was to make these companies financially secure and allow them to perform their critical functions without disruption.

Policymakers also understood the importance of bailing out vulnerable companies that were dealing with adverse liquidity conditions. Since the value chain was impacted by the lockdown, certain companies were unable to access payments from debtors, and this, in turn, delayed their payments to creditors. Companies were not only having trouble in their daily operations but also had problems paying salaries to their employees.

The introduction of the ₹2 lac crore ECLGS scheme was a move in the right direction and offered much-needed credit support to such companies. RBI was also instructed to delay the identification of defaulters while following its usual 30-day, 90-day, and 180-day defaulter identification program. At the same time, NBFCs with weak credit profiles were also provided with emergency liquidity support as these companies were unable to collect repayments due to borrower defaults.

Table 2: Atmanirbhar Bharat Abhiyan 2.0 (Government's COVID-19 Package Highlights).[11] Data sourced from Press Bureau (PIB), Government of India.

Recipient	Scheme	Quantum of Government Support
Ministry of Defence & Ministry of Road Transport	Additional Sanction for Capital Expenditure	₹25,000 crore
States (11 Nos.)	Interest-free Loans for Capital Expenditure	₹3,621 crore

11 Press Bureau | Government of India | Atmanirbhar Bharat Package Announcement | https://static.pib.gov.in/WriteReadData/userfiles/Atmanirbhar%20Package%203.0%20final%20final%20%20-%20Copy%201.pdf

Atmanirbhar 2.0 Stimulus Package closely followed Package 1.0 and was primarily focused on strengthening the operations of state-owned companies performing critical functions. Primary beneficiaries were the Ministry of Road Transport and the Ministry of Railways, which were instructed to go full steam ahead in the capital expenditure initiatives. This was necessary to create the necessary jobs, as well as create demand for basic and intermediate items, as well as capital goods. The Ministry of Defence was also pulled into action, considering Chinese aggression on the border, and it was important to build the necessary infrastructure on the border. Roughly ₹28,000 crore were allocated for the endeavour.

Table 3: Atmanirbhar Bharat Abhiyan 3.0 (Government COVID-19 Package Highlights).[12] Data sourced from Press Bureau (PIB), Government of India.

Recipient	Scheme	Quantum of Government Support
Industries Belonging to 26 Stressed Sectors (Including the Healthcare Sector) As Recommended by the Kamath Committee	Emergency Credit Line Guarantee Scheme (ECLGS) 2.0	₹1,00,000 crore Total Sanction for ECLGS 1.0 & 2.0: ₹3,00,000 crore
Employment Seekers & Aspiring Entrepreneurs	Rozgar Protsahan Yojana (PMRPY)	₹8,300 crore
Urban Homeowners	Housing for All (Pradhan Mantri Awaas Yojana – Urban)	₹18,000 crore
Mobile Manufacturing Active Pharmaceutical Ingredients (API) Medical Devices	Production Linked Incentive (PLI) 1.0	₹51,255 crore

12 Press Bureau | Government of India | Atmanirbhar Bharat Package Announcement | https://static.pib.gov.in/WriteReadData/userfiles/Atmanirbhar%20Package%20 3.0%20final%20final%20%20-%20Copy%201.pdf

Recipient	Scheme	Quantum of Government Support
Advance Cell Chemistry (ACC) Battery Electronic Products Auto & Ancillaries Pharmaceuticals Telecommunication Technology Textile Products Food Products Solar Panels (PVs) White Goods (Electronics) Specialized Steel	Production Linked Incentive (PLI) 2.0	₹1,46,000 crore
Exporters	EXIM Bank Support Program	₹3,000 crore
Vaccine Developers	COVID-19 Suraksha R&D Grant	₹900 crore
Rural Unemployed		₹18,000 crore
Defence Equipment Manufacturers		₹10,200 crore
Farmers	Fertilizer Subsidy	₹65,000 crore
Infrastructure Players	Equity Funding of NIIF	₹6,000 crore

Atmanirbhar 3.0 Stimulus Package was more comprehensive by nature as it covered several consumption-focused sectors, which were earlier left out of the government's priority list. The third package was worth around ₹2.65 lac crore and introduced incentives to not only potential homeowners but also infrastructure players, as well as potential investors. The government of India, by the end of 2020, realized that in a low-interest rate environment, it would be a wise idea to channel foreign investment into India via the foreign direct investment (FDI) route. Also, considering US and China tensions, a geopolitical shift was occurring in the world, as corporations and governments wanted to reduce their dependence on China, thereby diversifying their production lines.

India, being an equally large market and offering attractive growth and competitive tax rates, could be a viable alternative, and with this thought, the government of India pitched the ~₹2 lac crore Performance Linked Incentive (PLI) Scheme to potential investors, who were willing to set up manufacturing plants in India in special economic zones. Based on the size of their investment, the entering corporations were entitled to tax rebates and other incentives from the government of India.

The Atmanirbhar Package 3.0, therefore, focused on long-term job creation and capacity building, while taking care of the most pressing issues pertaining to vulnerable farmers (via the ₹65,000 crore fertilizer subsidy scheme) and rural unemployed (via extra cash infusion into the MGNREGA scheme). Also, unsold inventory build-up in the real estate segment meant that developers were facing high pressure from creditors. While the ECLGS scheme supported such developers, the government also provided subsidies to new home buyers in order to incentivize rapid inventory drawdowns in the housing segment.

At the same time, the ECLGS scheme was extended to 26 of the most vulnerable sectors of the economy. Renewed focus on domestic development of COVID-19 vaccines/inoculation led to the provision of ₹900 crore R&D fund for pharmaceutical majors.

Table 4: Atmanirbhar Bharat Abhiyan 4.0 (Government COVID-19 Package Highlights)[13] Q1 FY21–22. Data sourced from Press Bureau (PIB), Government of India.

Recipient	Scheme	Quantum of Government Support
Industries Belonging to Stressed Sectors	ECLGS 3.0	₹1,50,000 crore
Small Borrowers	Micro Finance Loans	₹7,500 crore
Healthcare Providers	Loan Guarantee Scheme	₹50,000 crore
Healthcare Providers	Paediatric Care (Fund for ICU Beds, Oxygen Equipment, and Professional Skilling & Recruitment)	₹23,220 crore

13 Cabinet Approves Covid Stimulus Package for ₹6.29 lac crores | The Economic Times | https://economictimes.indiatimes.com/news/economy/policy/cabinet-approves-rs-6-29-lakh-crore-covid-19-relief-package-announced-by-fm/articleshow/83985109.cms?from=mdr

Recipient	Scheme	Quantum of Government Support
Exporters		₹1,21,000 crore
Tourist Guides & Travel Agencies	Loan Guarantee Scheme	₹60,000 crore
Farmers	Fertilizer Subsidy	₹14,775 crore
Village Panchayats	Broadband Connection	₹19,041 crore
Exporters	Exporter Insurance Cover	₹88,000 crore

Atmanirbhar 4.0 Stimulus Package was introduced in the year 2021, in the month of June (Q1 FY22) and was worth around ₹4.8 lac crore (fiscal side) and around ₹2 lac crore (from the monetary side). As the economy had already dealt with one lockdown and was imminently facing another lockdown, the government of India expanded its support to include those involved in the tourist industry and healthcare providers. While the healthcare sector was provided with a fiscal support of around ₹73,000 crore, the tourist industry (including tourist guides) was provided with a support of ₹60,000 crore.

At the same time, fertilizer subsidy was further replenished with ₹14,775 crore, and a further ₹19,000 crore were provisioned for village panchayats to augment broadband capabilities. Exporters, who were deemed to be an important source of job creation as well as earners of the much-needed foreign exchange, were provided with a fiscal package worth over ₹1.5 lac crore (including insurance cover). For the support of vulnerable companies operating in other sectors, the support deadline of the ECLGS scheme was further extended.

Table 5: Atmanirbhar Bharat Abhiyan 5.0 (Government COVID-19 Package Highlights)[14] Announced in FY22–23. Data sourced from Press Bureau (PIB), Government of India.

Recipient	Scheme	Quantum of Government Support
Farmers	Fertilizer Subsidy	₹1,09,000 crore
Below Poverty Line (BPL) Families	Food Subsidy Pradhan Mantri Garib Kalyan Anna Yojana (PMGKAY)	₹80,348 crore
Oil Marketing Companies (OMCs)	Under-Recovery Compensation	₹24,944 crore
Infrastructure Companies Ministry of Railways Ministry of Road Transport and Highways (NHAI)	Infrastructure Capital Expenditure	>₹1,00,000 crore

The final Stimulus Package 5.0 came into effect in Q4 FY23. The package was estimated to be worth around ₹4.26 lac crore. Nevertheless, given robust tax receipts and the government's earlier savings, ₹1 lac crore is already provisioned for, and a parliamentary nod for just ₹3.26 lac crore (extra net borrowings) has been sought in December 2022. The package's primary focus remains on farmers and underprivileged classes of society (those belonging to the Below Poverty Line categories). It is expected to include a fertilizer subsidy of over ₹1 lac crore and over ₹80,000 crore as food subsidy for underprivileged families. Additionally, ₹29,000 crore have been allocated for subsidizing the operations of OMCs, which are operating in a highly vulnerable commodity (oil) market. An estimated

14 Government Seeks Parliamentary Approval | Parliament Nod Sought for Extra Spend of ₹3.25 lac crore on Subsidy and Capex | https://economictimes.indiatimes.com/news/economy/finance/govt-seeks-parliament-nod-for-net-additional-spending-of-rs-3-25-lakh-cr-this-fiscal/articleshow/96106019.cms

₹1 lac crore + will be allocated for the development of the ongoing infrastructure scheme, including the 'Pradhan Mantri Gati Shakti Project'. These high-value projects are critical to India's dream of becoming a $10 trillion economy by FY32–33.

Table 6: Total Stimulus Packages (All Packages).[15]

Package	Quantum Allocated (₹ Cr.)
Atmanirbhar Bharat Abhiyan 1.0	₹11,02,650 crore
Atmanirbhar Bharat Abhiyan 2.0	₹73,000 crore
Atmanirbhar Bharat Abhiyan 3.0	₹2,65,080 crore
Atmanirbhar Bharat Abhiyan 4.0	₹4,79,000 crore
Atmanirbhar Bharat Abhiyan 5.0	₹4,26,000 crore
Pradhan Mantri Garib Kalyan Yojana (PMGJY) Phase 1 & 2	₹2,75,000 crore
Total	₹26,20,000 crore

Table 7: Monetary and Fiscal Combined Packages Estimates.

Support Provided by the RBI Estimated	~ ₹17,00,000 crore
RBI Dividends (FY20–FY22)	~₹1,86,000 crore
Total (Fiscal + Monetary Packages)	~ ₹45,06,000 crore
Percentage of Indian GDP (FY22–23)	~16.5%

15 Press Bureau | Government of India | Atmanirbhar Bharat Package Announcement | https://static.pib.gov.in/WriteReadData/userfiles/Atmanirbhar%20Package%20 3.0%20final%20final%20%20-%20Copy%201.pdf

Cabinet Approves Covid Stimulus Package for ₹6.29 lac crore | The Economic Times | https://economictimes.indiatimes.com/news/economy/policy/cabinet-approves-rs-6-29-lakh-crore-covid-19-relief-package-announced-by-fm/articleshow/83985109.cms?from=mdr

Government Seeks Parliamentary Approval | Parliament Nod Sought for Extra Spend of ₹3.25 lac crore on Subsidy and Capex | https://economictimes.indiatimes.com/news/economy/finance/govt-seeks-parliament-nod-for-net-additional-spending-of-rs-3-25-lakh-cr-this-fiscal/articleshow/96106019.cms

Overall, India's fiscal response to the COVID-19 pandemic to support a flailing economy is estimated to be roughly ₹26.2 lac crore. This figure not only includes the 5 Atmanirbhar Bharat Stimulus Packages but also the ₹2.75 lac crore worth Pradhan Mantri Garib Kalyan Yojana (PMGKY), introduced immediately after the initiation of national lockdowns in March 2020. While including the RBI's monetary support of an estimated ₹17 lac crore in liquidity support to the economy, the total stimulus comes to about ₹45.06 lac crore. Since these numbers include stimulus packages between calendar years 2020–2022, the combined numbers are utilized to reach a percentage of nominal GDP figure of 16.5 per cent. Given the multi-quarter spread of the packages, an annual assessment (with prevalent annual GDP) did not make sense during the analysis. Benchmarking FY22–23 nominal GDP to this author's estimates best served the purpose, primarily because the year represented a somewhat recovered economy, and convincingly covered a 3-year build-up of stimulus packages from both the monetary and fiscal sides.

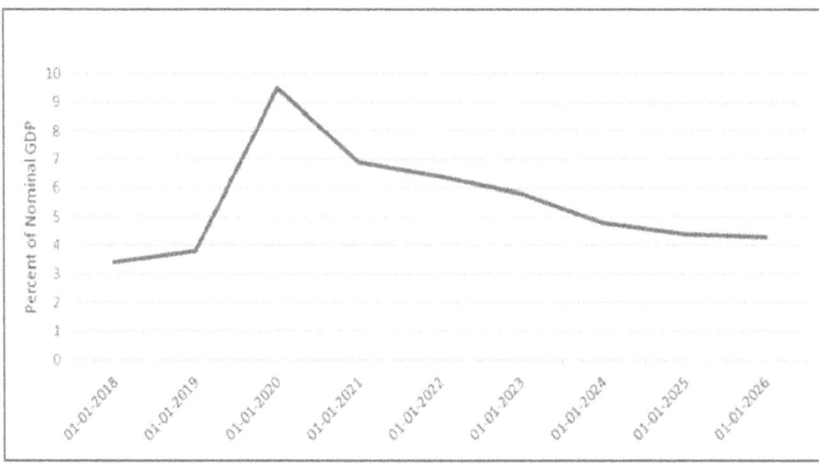

India Fiscal Deficit Evolution (as a % of Nominal GDP)

Figure 1: The evolution of the fiscal deficit during the COVID years, and the estimated dynamic.

Data sourced from Macrobond.

Table 8: Government of India Fiscal Position FY20–21 to FY21–22 (in ₹Crore.).[16] Sourced from Union Budget documents and the author's estimates.

Head	FY20–21 (BE)	FY20–21 (RE)	FY21–22 (BE)
Total Receipts	30,42,230 (+13% YoY)	34,50,305 (+28% YoY)	34,83,236 (+14%YoY)
Capital Expenditure	4,12,085 (+18% YoY)	4,39,163 (+30% YoY)	5,54,236 (+34%YoY)
Total Expenditure	30,42,230 (+13% YoY)	34,50,305 (+28% YoY)	34,83,236 (+14%YoY)
Fiscal Deficit	7,96,337 (+4% YoY)	18,48,655 (+98% YoY)	15,06,812 (+89%YoY)
Net Debt Raised	5,40,870 (+8% YoY)	13,83,683 (+187%YoY)	9,34,565 (+73%YoY)
Gross Borrowings	10,29,714 (+11% YoY)	18,28,564 (+97% YoY)	12,05,500 (+17%YoY)
Interest Payment Obligations	7,08,203 (+13% YoY)	6,92,900 (+13% YoY)	8,09,701 (+14%YoY)
Tax Receipts	16,35,909 (+9% YoY)	13,44,501 (−1% YoY)	15,45,396 (−6% YoY)

Table 9: Government of India Fiscal Position FY21–22 to FY22–23 (in ₹ Crore) Cont.

Head	FY21–22 (RE)	FY22–23 (BE)
Total Receipts	37,70,000	39,44,909 (+13% YoY)
Capital Expenditure	6,02,711	7,50,246 (+35% YoY)

(*Continued*)

16 India Budget Statistics | https://www.indiabudget.gov.in/

Table 9: (*Continued*)

Head	FY21–22 (RE)	FY22–23 (BE)
Total Expenditure	37,70,000	39,44,909 (+13% YoY)
Fiscal Deficit	15,91,089	16,61,196 (+10% YoY)
Net Debt Raised	12,00,000	11,59,000 (+24% YoY)
Gross Borrowings	15,85,823	14,95,000 (+24% YoY)
Interest Payment Obligations	8,13,791	9,40,651 (+16% YoY)
Tax Receipts	17,65,145	19,34,771 (+25% YoY)

It is also important to discuss the source of financing this massive fiscal exercise and budget, as well as revised estimates of the Ministry of Finance, which sheds light on the subject. It is estimated that in response to the COVID-19 pandemic, the government of India's net borrowings increased by ₹8.4 lac crore over and above the original budget estimate for the FY21 financial year. While tax receipts were lower by an estimated ₹3 lac crore, total expenditure was over ₹4 lac crore above the budget estimate. Consequently, the fiscal deficit was over ₹10 lac crore higher than the budget estimate (estimated at over 9 per cent of GDP in revised estimate) and was partly utilized to compensate for lost tax income, given the lockdown and the resulting lower household consumption.

The Government's renewed focus on capital expenditure to drive economic growth (when all else failed to fire cylinders) resulted in an incremental expenditure in the category of ₹27,000 crore as per the revised budgetary estimates for 2020–21. Such was the impetus on the category that the expenditure grew from ₹4.39 lac crore as per revised estimates for 2020–21, to over ₹7.5 lac crore as per budgetary estimates for 2022–23. This happened despite the fact that total receipts normalized to ₹39.4 lac crore (BE 2022–23), from ₹34.4 lac crore (during the COVID year 2020–21 RE). It can be argued that capex helped in stabilizing the economy, sustaining job growth, and driving demand for the primary/core sectors.

This was, nevertheless, at the cost of unsustainable interest payment obligations that rose from ₹6.93 lac crore (as per RE 2020–21), to ₹9.4 lac crore (as per BE 2022–23). This was aided by normalizing interest rates as galloping inflation (especially core) started to become sticky. As a matter of fact, the Repo rate normalized by 250 bps between May 2022 and February 2023. Consequently, interest obligations as a percentage of total expenditure rose from 20 per cent in 2020–21 RE to 24 per cent in 2022–23 BE. This had an adverse impact on other welfare expenditure, which had implications for vulnerable groups/households in the economy, that may have required help during this time. This was especially true given the fact that incremental obligations could not be compensated with incremental fiscal deficit, because of stringent FRB Mandates (despite remaining elusive during much of the COVID era).

Answering the policy question, based on the data presented, and the Government's assessment of the macroeconomic situation, it can be argued that packaged so presented were indeed all encompassing, and covered a lot of ground quickly. While the Government was concerned about its mounting debt to GDP ratio, as well as fiscal deficit target breaching the FRBM by several notches (normalization pushing back consolidation by a few years), fiscal reaction cannot be faulted. Nevertheless, resources were never mobilized to help the most vulnerable families in the country. Most peers did offer helicopter money to households (in coordination with their respective central banks), but not India. This was a lost opportunity, and a fiscal package worth at least 3 per cent of GDP could have been offered to 50 million (out of a total of 296 million) most vulnerable households during the financial year 2020–21.

CHAPTER 4

India's Monetary Response to COVID-19

Policy Question: Was the Monetary Response Adequate for a Crisis?

RBI's monetary response started with an out-of-turn policy meeting scheduled on 27th March 2020. In this meeting, the RBI's MPC, slashed the Repo Rate by 75 bps,[17] bringing the rate to 4.4 per cent. On 22nd May 2020, the MPC further reduced the Repo rate by 40 bps, bringing the rate to 4 per cent.[18] Initially, the primary objective of the RBI was to sustain the economy at all costs, and economic growth gained prominence over inflation management.

This level was maintained until May 2022, and monetary policy remained accommodative, with the RBI infusing liquidity into the system. The Cash Reserve Ratio (CRR) was also slashed by 100 bps to 3 per cent[19] of Net Deposit Time Liability (NDTL), unleashing over ₹1 lac crore of incremental liquidity into the banking system.

The RBI ended FY20 with a Balance Sheet size of ₹53.3 lac crore,[20] expanding by over 30 per cent, as compared to 13.4 per cent the previous year. CIC, in turn, expanded by 21.5 per cent,[21] compared to over 13.4 per cent growth recorded

17 Bank Bazar | Repo Rate Movement | https://www.bankbazaar.com/home-loan/repo-rate.html

18 Bank Bazar | Repo Rate Movement | https://www.bankbazaar.com/home-loan/repo-rate.html

19 Banking System to be Flushed with Liquidity as CRR cut to 3% | The Hindu Business Line | https://www.thehindubusinessline.com/money-and-banking/banking-system-will-be-flush-with-liquidity-as-crr-cut-to-3-per-cent/article31178978.ece

20 Banking Data | RBI Balance Sheet | RBI Annual Report | https://annualreport.rbi.org.in/

21 Banking Data | RBI Balance Sheet | RBI Annual Report | https://annualreport.rbi.org.in/

the previous year. However, as lockdown ensued and households were unable to indulge in consumption, free cash therefore translated into savings. This resulted in Deposits expanding by over 53.7 per cent[22] despite a cut in CRR.

Due to global turmoil and resultant volatility, USD and Gold appreciated in value, and therefore, these holdings on the RBI's assets recorded an upward revision. Quick rate reductions by the US Federal Reserve also fed into US Treasuries, appreciating valuations. Consequently, the Net Foreign Assets appreciated by 23.7 per cent[23] by the end of FY20 as compared to just over 2 per cent appreciation recorded the previous year. The revaluation account (which records the appreciation or depreciation of reserve assets on the liability side of the RBI's balance sheet), as a result, expanded by over 30 per cent.[24]

As part of the monetary support within the stimulus package announced by the government, the RBI revised the identification guidelines for the SMAs and Non-Performing Accounts (NPA). This was done to give a much-needed fillip to commercial banks, which were under pressure from mounting provisioning costs in the light of poor-performing borrower companies. The ₹2 lac crore plus Emergency Credit Line Guarantee Scheme (ECLGS) was also made available to the most vulnerable sectors of the economy and later extended to 26 such sectors.[25] The purpose of the scheme was to protect companies from collapsing during the lockdown period and numerous uncertainties, which, in a normal case, would have destabilized the economy.

Credit facilities and special windows were also made available to the NBFCs, including Micro Finance Institutions (MFIs), as their credit profiles deteriorated in the light of borrower delinquencies. A special window was also provided to the fixed-income space as yields skyrocketed and investors (both institutional and non-institutional) were unable to trade these assets in the open market.

22 Banking Data | RBI Balance Sheet | RBI Annual Report | https://annualreport.rbi.org.in/

23 Banking Data | RBI Balance Sheet | RBI Annual Report | https://annualreport.rbi.org.in/

24 Banking Data | RBI Balance Sheet | RBI Annual Report | https://annualreport.rbi.org.in/

25 Press Bureau | Government of India | Atmanirbhar Bharat Package Announcement | https://static.pib.gov.in/WriteReadData/userfiles/Atmanirbhar%20Package%203.0%20final%20final%20%20-%20Copy%201.pdf

Table 10: RBI Balance Sheet Snapshot from Actual, Growth, and Proportions Perspectives. Data sourced from RBI data, and the author's calculations.

Actual[26]					
	Balance Sheet (INR Cr.)@	CIC (INR Cr.)@	CRR@*	Deposits	Revaluation Account
FY19	41,02,905	21,68,797	5,65,000	7,64,922	8,61,817*
FY20	53,34,792	26,35,575	5,36,000	11,75,860	11,24,391
FY21	57,07,669	28,26,862	5,42,000	14,91,537	9,24,455
FY22	61,90,302	31,05,720	6,83,000	17,33,787	9,34,544
FY23	63,44,756	33,48,244	8,69,000	13,54,217	11,26,088
FY24	70,47,703	34,78,039	10,08,000	17,19,838	11,30,963

*@Revised Estimate *Estimated*

Growth

	Balance Sheet	CIC@	CRR	Deposits	Revaluation Account
FY19	13.42%	13.43%	7.48%	17.21%	11.10%
FY20	30.02%	21.52%	−5.13%	53.72%	30.47%
FY21	6.99%	7.26%	1.12%	26.85%	−17.78%
FY22	8.46%	9.86%	26.01%	16.24%	1.09%
FY23	2.50%	7.81%	27.23%	−21.89%	20.50%
FY24	11.08%	3.88%	16.00%	27.00%	0.43%

Proportions

	Balance Sheet	CIC@	CRR	Deposits	Revaluation Account
FY19	100%	52.86%	13.77%	18.64%	21.01%
FY20	100%	49.40%	10.05%	22.04%	21.08%
FY21	100%	49.53%	9.50%	26.13%	16.20%
FY22	100%	50.17%	11.03%	28.01%	15.10%
FY23	100%	52.77%	13.70%	21.34%	17.75%
FY24	100%	49.35%	12.33%	24.40%	16.05%

Note: CRR: Cash Reserve Ratio; CIC: Currency in Circulation

26 RBI Data: https://www.rbi.org.in/Scripts/AnnualReportPublications.aspx?year=2024

Overall, for most of FY21, the system liquidity was around ₹4 lac crore[27] (as estimated by the RBI's Weekly Reverse Repo Operations) on average, and this kept the call money rate (described by the WACR) in the lower vicinity of the policy/monetary corridor.

As the government of India increased its net debt issuance almost three-fold, the RBI had to engage in deficit financing in line with the Hicks–Hanson Model. Accordingly, the RBI's balance sheet continued to expand but at a sub-optimal 7 per cent in FY21 (revised balance sheet estimate), nonetheless. This happened because inflation began to take hold over the global economy, and taper tantrum-type symptoms were evident in the capital markets across the world. Consequently, yields stabilized upwards, shedding valuation gains of the previous few quarters. The proportion of net domestic asset (NDA) holdings (government securities), thanks to net domestic borrowings – increased to 23 per cent of the balance sheet, and this lent the expansion in the overall balance sheet.

A point to be noted is that despite the volatility emanating from foreign sources, this rise in proportion of domestic assets was 2 per cent higher than the assets' proportion in FY20.

Still, on average, foreign portfolio investors net invested ₹2.6 lac crore[28] in the Indian capital market in FY21 (the primary pandemic year), compared to net (–) ₹0.27 lac crore,[29] withdrawn during the previous year. Nevertheless, monetary loosening in the rest of the world meant that yield-chasing capital from the developed markets such as the United States, European Union, and Japan funnelled into Indian capital markets. India recorded a record FDI inflow of $84.8 billion in FY21 alone,[30] and this led to the accumulation of a large amount of foreign assets on the RBI's balance sheet. As a result, the net foreign assets continued to expand by over 18.5 per cent in

27 RBI Weekly Data for years | 2020 | 2021 https://rbi.org.in/Scripts/BS_ViewWSS.aspx

28 India Biggest Recipient of FPI Inflows Worth ₹2.6 lac crore in FY21 | Deccan Herald | https://www.deccanherald.com/business/business-news/india-biggest-recipient-of-fpi-inflows-worth-rs-26-lakh-crore-in-fy21-968701.html

29 India Biggest Recipient of FPI Inflows Worth ₹2.6 lac crore in FY21 | Deccan Herald | https://www.deccanherald.com/business/business-news/india-biggest-recipient-of-fpi-inflows-worth-rs-26-lakh-crore-in-fy21-968701.html

30 India FDI Policy | Invest India | https://www.investindia.gov.in/foreign-direct-investment

much of FY21. Since an expanding reserve asset holding necessitated the issuance of currency, the CIC expanded by 7.3 per cent (albeit at almost half the pre-pandemic rate), despite a contracting economy. As a proportion of the balance sheet, net foreign assets were recorded at 69 per cent (highest in recent history), and the RBI ended the FY21 with a balance sheet size of ₹57 lac crore (recording a growth when the GDP contracted by over −7 per cent). FY22 began with strong consumer demand on the back of lifting restrictions. As a result, inflationary tendencies began to build up in the global and national economy, and volatility began the rile the markets.

Consequently, the households were sceptical of the economy's capacity to sustain in the medium term, and inflation expectations (as measured by the RBI's Inflation Expectation Surveys) demonstrated this insecurity. At the same time, industries were also unsure about the economic ground realities and were therefore unwilling to invest in capacity expansion as utilization levels (as per the RBI's OBICUS surveys) remained sub-par. Nevertheless, the fiscal muscle continued to be flexed and resulted in continued monetization of debt. As a consequence, a growth of almost 9.9 per cent was recorded by CIC.

This resulted in lower credit offtake than previously anticipated, and therefore, the rate of deposit growth was still faster than the rate of credit growth. Despite the situation, credit offtake managed a faster run than the previous year, and the CRR account of the RBI expanded by over 26 per cent by the end of FY22. Since the previous year's expansion was just 1.1 per cent, the account representing the central bank's statutory requirement appeared to be more amplified than actual reality.

Overall deposits, which included the Reverse Repo Operations (representing the account that embody the RBI's accumulation of cash borrowed from commercial banks in exchange of government securities), also expanded by over 16.2 per cent and its proportion to the RBI's balance sheet expanded to over 28 per cent (again highest in recent history) by the end of FY22, as compared to 26 per cent in FY21.

Global volatility and taper tantrums (the US Fed's aggressive commentary pertaining to rates) resulted in a somewhat slower growth in foreign portfolio money. This resulted in the net foreign assets declining to 67 per cent as a proportion of the RBI's balance sheet and expanding by just around 7.5 per cent by the end of FY22, as compared to 18.5 per cent growth recorded the previous year. Overall, the RBI ended the year with a balance sheet size of ₹61.9 lac crore, representing an expansion of around 8.5 per cent.

FY23 was very different, with inflation fast becoming galloping and preceding growth. Monetary tightening took over the place from monetary easing, and the financial year witnessed hikes of 250 bps[31], taking the benchmark Repo Rate to 6.50 per cent from 4.0 per cent, a year earlier. This closely followed what was happening elsewhere, especially in the developed markets, where key central banks such as the US Federal Reserve, the European Central Bank (ECB), and the Bank of Japan (BOJ) were busy tightening (more aggressively) or in the process of tightening their respective monetary policies.

Given the circumstances, the average differentials between the rate of return (both cost of equity and the average return on debt instruments) offered by India (like other emerging markets) and that offered by a developed market declined. Moreover, this happened primarily because India's RBI was slower in raising rates as compared to, for example, the US Federal Reserve.

Also, the depletion due to the selling of 'a part' of foreign reserves by the RBI to protect the Indian Rupee from depreciation against the USD, which gained strength amidst volatility, started to become a cause for concern.

In total, the RBI had sold nearly ₹4 lac core worth of foreign assets towards the end of that financial year. This resulted in the contraction of the Revaluation account by (−) 7.5 per cent, and foreign asset holdings have gone down by (−) 8.3 per cent, until the end of three quarters of FY23.

As CIC must be backed up 100 per cent by foreign assets (by the issuing department of the RBI), the account representing CIC grew by just over 2.6 per cent until the start of Q4, on the back of contracting reserve holdings. However, appreciation and incremental accretion of gold holdings backstopped the declines, and the CIC account expanded by a little over 7.8 per cent.

Notwithstanding, the financial year ending balance sheet (revised estimates) expanded by just over 2.5 per cent, aided by a strong appreciation in the revaluations towards the end of Q4.

As the balance sheet normalized to somewhat pre-COVID levels, credit offtake was seen increasing significantly on the back of government-driven capital expenditure and subsidy schemes for rural households/ farmers in FY23.

31 Bank Bazar | Repo Rate Movement | https://www.bankbazaar.com/home-loan/repo-rate.html

This phenomenon increased demand for cash amidst the RBI's absorption of liquidity (on average ₹5–7 lac crore on a weekly basis), leading to contraction of the deposit account by (−) 21.9 per cent. What this means is that the RBI's Reverse Repo Operations (under the larger Liquidity Adjustment Facility, LAF) have received a lower response from commercial banks, as they struggle to meet demand for credit. At the same time, as consumption has returned, growth in deposits has been declining since Q2 FY23. This was in turn demonstrated by a CRR growth of over 27 per cent, overall, in FY23, almost the same as compared to the account's recording in the previous year's closing.

Overall, the RBI started Q3 FY23 with a balance sheet size of ₹58.5 lac crore, which is a contraction of (−) 6.6 per cent, but finally managed to end the year with a size of ₹63.4 lac crore (expansion of 2.5 per cent), thanks to the reasons stated above. This metric was, of course, one of the lowest expansions in recent history.

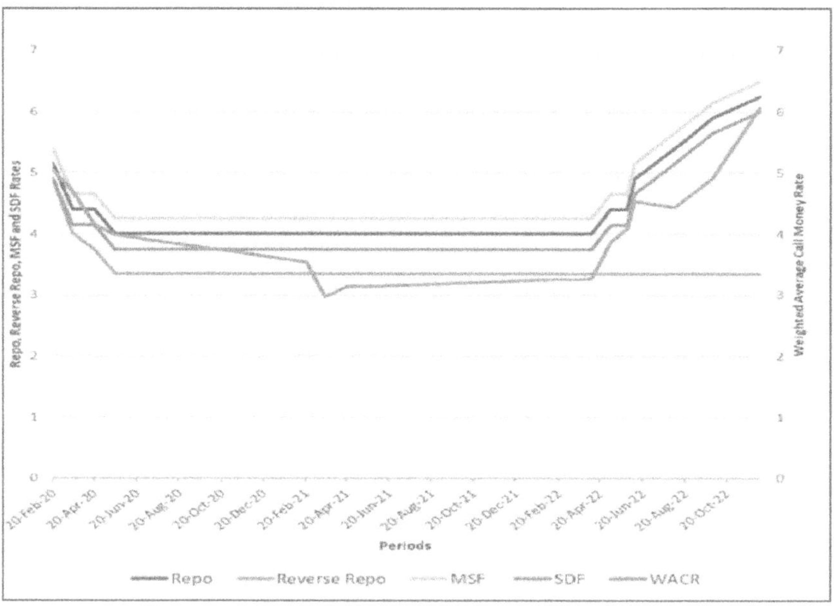

RBI MONETARY CORRIDOR

Figure 2: Depiction of the evolving monetary corridor during the COVID period.

Data sourced from RBI & Macrobond.

As the RBI has begun tightening the monetary policy amidst rising inflationary tendencies in the economy, pressures have been felt in the overnight call money market (WACR).

WACR is the rate that represents the money market rate at which commercial banks borrow from each other overnight without collateral (borrowing without the need for government securities as collateral). The WACR is therefore the lowest rate in the Indian monetary system (and is only above the Reverse Repo Rate) and is the first to get impacted when commercial banks face liquidity pressures.

Consequently, whenever the WACR is near the upper threshold of the MSF, which, in turn, is the highest borrowing rate in the system, it means that commercial banks are facing a liquidity crunch. On the other hand, when the WACR is near the Reverse Repo Rate threshold, it means that commercial banks are in a comfortable liquidity scenario.

Therefore, a neutral policy stance in the RBI's parlance signifies that the WACR must remain somewhere in the middle of this policy/ monetary corridor. In the meantime, the RBI introduced a fourth component of the corridor by the name of Standard Deposit Facility (SDF). The SDF is the second-lowest hurdle rate of the monetary system and has since replaced the Reverse Repo Rate as the lower bound of the corridor.

Therefore, when the RBI started its monetary tightening, the WACR was the first to be impacted. By 6th May 2022, the WACR increased to 3.87 per cent,[32] as compared to 3.27 per cent recorded a month earlier. It must be noted that the call money rate was even below the Reverse Repo Rate for much of FY21 and FY22 amidst a liquidity glut in the system, and its sudden increase came as a shock for small commercial banks, which had to then borrow at a higher rate to meet their daily operational needs.

As of 7th December 2022, the WACR was recorded at 6.07 per cent,[33] which was just 18 bps (100 bps = 1 per cent) lower than the Repo Rate itself. For reference, the Repo Rate – WACR differential was recorded at 103 bps back in March 2021. Tightening liquidity conditions have therefore become the new reality, and the RBI is expected to further raise rates (along with

32 RBI Weekly Statistical Supplement | https://rbi.org.in/Scripts/BS_ViewWSS.aspx

33 RBI Weekly Statistical Supplement | https://rbi.org.in/Scripts/BS_ViewWSS.aspx

absorption of excess cash from the banking system) well in Q4 FY23, to anchor inflationary expectations.

Clearly, inflation control has now taken precedence over economic growth for the RBI and its MPC as we head towards the middle of FY25.

Overall, considering the multiple liquidity infusion operations as well as providing other liquidity support and guarantees to vulnerable businesses, the RBI has provided an estimated total liquidity support of around ₹15 lac crore[34] since the start of the pandemic.

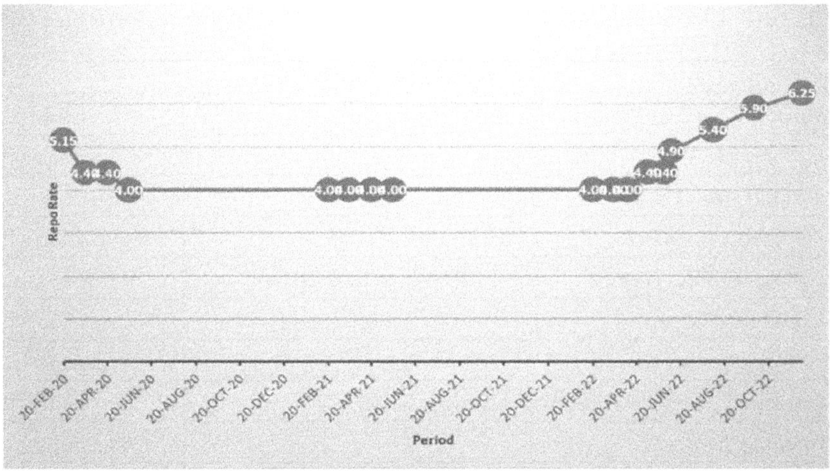

Repo Rate (in bps)

Figure 3: Depicting the Repo Rate evolution during the COVID period.
Data sourced from RBI & Macrobond.

In terms of the components of the monetary package, major details became available in the June 2021 RBI Bulletin. The components included TLTRO, Long Term Repo Operations (TLTRO), Term Repo & Variable Repo Facilities, OMO Operations, Statutory Liquidity Facility (SLR) cuts, and CRR cuts. In total, the estimated liquidity provisions can be estimated to be around ~₹17 lac crore. According to the compilation and assessment of the monetary response data, economist Jiji T Mathew of the National Institute

34 Author's Estimates Based on Government of India Data

of Bank Management (NIBM), the system eventually availed roughly 58 per cent of these facilities by the end of the FY2021–22. The lower-than-sanctioned scenario suggests that sufficient liquidity was provisioned and that the economic recovery was faster than previously anticipated. Facilities were provided to commercial banks and government-owned financial institutions that were dedicated to the upliftment of critical sectors. Special windows were also opened for mutual funds and NBFCs, and liquidity provisions were provided via commercial banks as facilitators of the system.

Table 11: Jiji T Mathew, NIBM (2022). Liquidity Facilities and Windows Provided by the RBI to the System[35]

Variable Repo Rate Facility	2,25,000*
Cut in CRR	1,37,000
TLTRO 1 & 2 Facility	1,50,000
Net OMO Purchases	3,70,000
On-Tap TLTRO Facility	1,00,000
LTRO Facility	2,00,000
56-Day Term Repo Facility	1,00,000
Emergency Health Services Access Facility (Term)	50,000
Cut in SLR (by 1%)	1,37,000
Special Liquidity Facility for Mutual Funds	50,000
NABARD, SIDBI, EXIM Bank Refinancing Facilities	1,41,000
Other Liquidity Facilities	~40,000
Total	~17,00,000

*Source: Jiji T Mathew, National Institute of Bank Management (NIBM); *in INR Crore.*

35 RBI's Post Covid Monetary and Liquidity Measures: Impact on Money, Bond, and Credit Markets (NIBM: Jiji T Mathew, 2022) https://www.nibmindia.org/static/working_paper/NIBM_WP19_JM.pdf

Impetus for the Fiscal Side from RBI Dividends

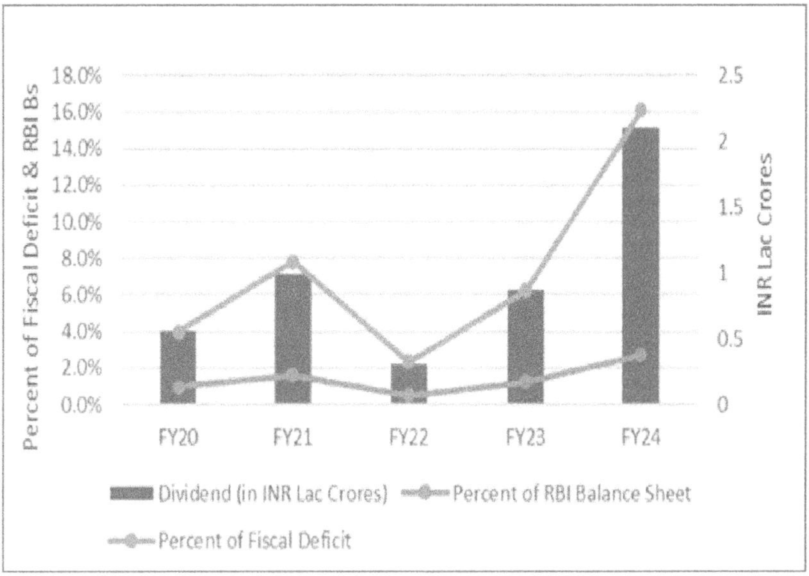

The Power of RBI Dividends

Figure 4: Depicting the evolution of the annual RBI dividends accessed by the Government of India.

Data sourced from RBI reports.

The RBI is rarely credited for creating enviable resources for the fiscal side, and the dividends paid on an annual basis have generally gone a long way in plugging general revenue gaps. As a public institution, while the RBI is obligated to pay dividends to the Government of India from its surpluses, under Section 47 of the RBI Act, 1934,[36] the transfer per se has never been a big deal in the grand scheme of things, especially after substantial tax growth thanks to the GST implementation. During a crisis like COVID, however, public capex remains the backbone of economic recovery, and in

36 RBI Surplus Transfer to the Government of India (Dristi IAS, 2024) https://www.drishtiias.com/daily-updates/daily-news-analysis/rbi-surplus-transfer-to-government

times like these, the importance of RBI dividends becomes a moot point for fiscal consolidators.

The first of these 'rainy-day' dividends came in 2020 for FY2019–20, and amounted to ₹56,000 crore. Since this amount was available for budget FY2020–21 (given the fact that dividends are usually paid in the first quarter of the following fiscal year), the amount made available to the Government of India was equivalent to 3 per cent of the revised estimate fiscal deficit for the year, and represented 1 per cent of the RBI's balance sheet. Thanks to substantial revaluation gains, the dividend paid for the FY2020–21 was a substantial ₹99,000 crore, and amounted to 6.2 per cent of the revised estimate fiscal deficit for FY2021–22, and represented 1.6 per cent of the RBI's balance sheet for the year. This also marked a marked growth in the devolution of the contingency account, and the RBI convinced the market that it was fairly confident about its balance sheet's ability to manage systemic volatility, if the need arises. FY2021–22 dividends were plagued by volatility caused by taper tantrums and resulted in substantial revaluation losses. This resulted in dividends paid being just ₹31,000 crore (a decline of 69 per cent YoY). This amounted to just 1.9 per cent of the revised estimate fiscal deficit for FY2022–23, and represented just 0.5 per cent of the RBI's balance sheet for the year.

In totality, the three-year dividends amounted to ₹1.86 lac crore of fiscal support, and were equivalent to over ~3.5 per cent of the fiscal deficit on average.

The RBI response was adequate, and the reaction function quickly refocused on growth maximization from inflation control. Liquidity support, and reserve management also remained satisfactory. Support to fiscal effort from the RBI in terms of dividends also averaged over 3.5 per cent of fiscal deficit, over a 3-year period (calendar year 2020–2022).

CHAPTER 5

Results of the Combined Macro Economic Response

Policy Question: How Successful was the Fiscal-Monetary Coordination?

The Indian economy recorded a contraction of 23.8 per cent in real terms in Q1 FY21.[37] This was the first contraction in decades, and COVID-induced lockdowns crippled the economy as household consumption was severely limited and 70–80 per cent of all industrial activity ceased momentarily. The fiscal response was primarily in the form of a revised debt issuance calendar and consequent growth in total expenditure. In turn, the RBI's reduction in interest rates meant that the government's interest obligation (on the back of higher debt issuance) was sustainable. Therefore, the government of India borrowed ₹8.4 lac crore (+187 per cent growth over the Revised Budget Estimate for FY20)[38] additionally. Consequently, the Fiscal Deficit expanded by over ₹11 lac crore (+98 per cent) for FY21 and was utilized by the government to offset its tax foregone losses and required public-funded capex and subsidies in order to sustain the economy. The RBI, on its part, monetized the incremental debt issued, with its net domestic debt holdings expanding by almost 28 per cent in FY21 as compared to just 13 per cent recorded the previous year. In other words, the RBI held ₹10.4 lac crore (₹1.2 lac crore incrementally)[39] of government securities on its balance sheet as reserves, as compared ₹9.2 lac crore in

37 Trading Economics | India GDP Annual Growth Rate | https://tradingeconomics.com/india/gdp-growth-annual

38 India Budget Statistics | https://www.indiabudget.gov.in/

39 Banking Data | RBI Balance Sheet | RBI Annual Report | https://annualreport.rbi.org.in/

the previous year. The proportion of such holdings on the balance sheet was also increased to 23 per cent (from 21 per cent) in FY21 by the RBI and further increased to 24 per cent as on Q3 FY23.[40]

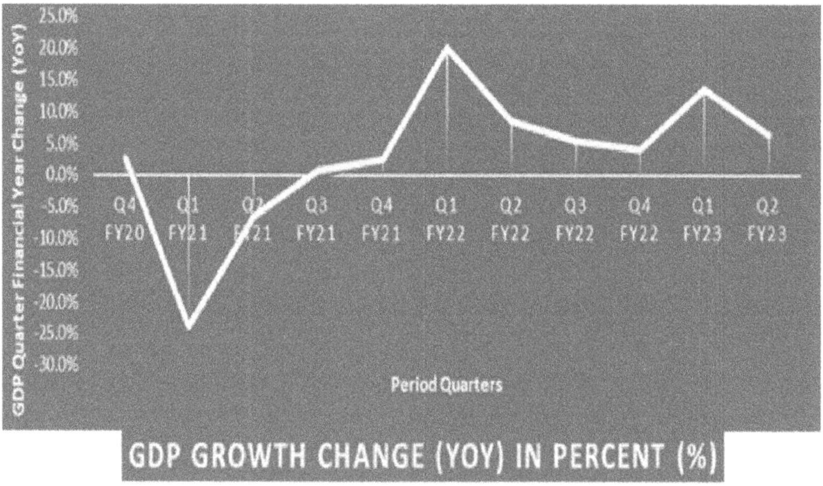

Figure 5: Depicting the GDP quarterly change (YoY) during the COVID period. *Data sourced from RBI & Ministry of Statistics Data.*

CIC, on the other hand, increased by 7.3 per cent in FY21, as capital inflows allowed RBI to build significant buffers in terms of foreign reserves and monetizing Indian government debt, providing an additional fillip.

CIC therefore grew to ₹28.3 lac crore by the end of FY21, as compared to ₹26.3 lac crore the previous year. However, lower than expected credit offtake and a consistently rising growth in deposits led to a situation where a significant proportion of the incremental CIC was deposited back to the RBI through the Reverse Repo Operations. This reduced the RBI's ability to issue more currency, as its liability side was taken over by an expanding deposit account.

40 Banking Data | RBI Balance Sheet | RBI Annual Report | https://annualreport.rbi.org.in/

Consequently, towards the end of FY22, while RBI's deposit account increased to ₹17.3 lac crore (additional ₹5.5 lac crore since the end of FY20), the CIC increased by just around ₹4.7 lac crore.[41]

CRR, which was 3 per cent of the NDTL, continued to grow as a proportion of the RBI's balance sheet on account of increased public deposits with commercial banks. As per the regulations, these commercial banks had to deposit 3 per cent of any incremental deposit with the RBI under the CRR account.

Despite the slow growth in CIC, inflation became a major problem in the economy since FY22, as the economy has somewhat normalized. Global tightening of monetary policy and the resultant impact on global capital movement forced the RBI to raise rates, increasing the cost of capital in the process.

At the same time, the breaking out of the Russia-Ukraine War jolted the commodity markets, especially since sanctions on Russia took out necessary supplies of certain Russian commodities supplies such as Crude, Wheat and other precious metals. This resulted in inflationary tendencies building up not only in India but all over the world. Inflation, as demonstrated by the Consumer Price Index (CPI), started its elevation in June 2020 (Q2 FY21) onwards, when it was recorded at 6.23 per cent. Significant government expenditure and deficit financing glutted the system with incremental currency issued (FY21) and logistics issues (due to lockdowns).

The government of India's gross debt increased by 97 per cent (or ₹ 8 lac crore incrementally) for FY21 (Revised Estimate), and a reduced rollover increased net debt by 187 per cent (or ₹8.4 lac crore). Total expenditure too went up by 28 per cent (or by ₹4 lac crore), while the economy contracted (−) 23.8 per cent in Q1 FY21 and (−) 6.6 per cent in Q2 FY21, in real terms.[42]

The rising public expenditure (through deficit financing), rising accumulation of foreign reserves, and contracting GDP caused an anomaly, which resulted in structural inflation. Inflation was, however, first infested in the WPI, which represents prices at the wholesale level and steadily made its way to the CPI, negatively impacting household consumption power.

41 Banking Data | RBI Balance Sheet | RBI Annual Report | https://annualreport.rbi.org.in/

42 India Budget Statistics | https://www.indiabudget.gov.in/

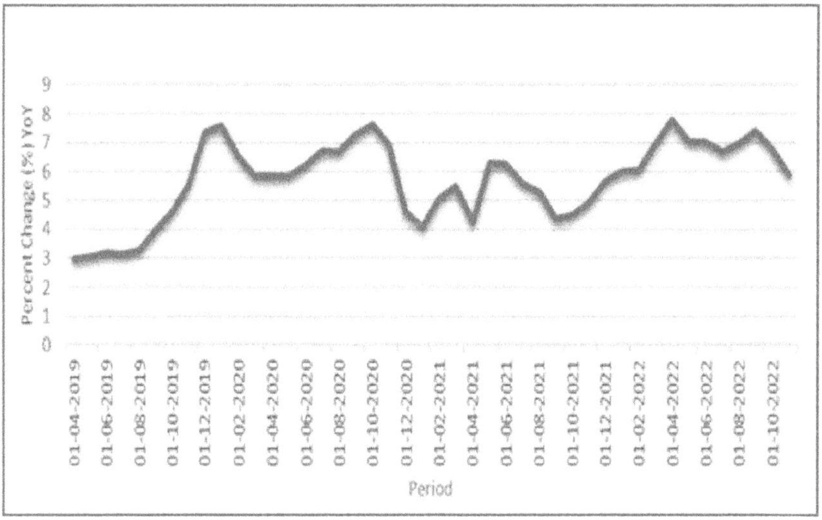

India Headline CPI (Consumer Inflation)

Figure 6: Sourced from RBI Data. Depicting the evolution of the Headline CPI during the COVID period.

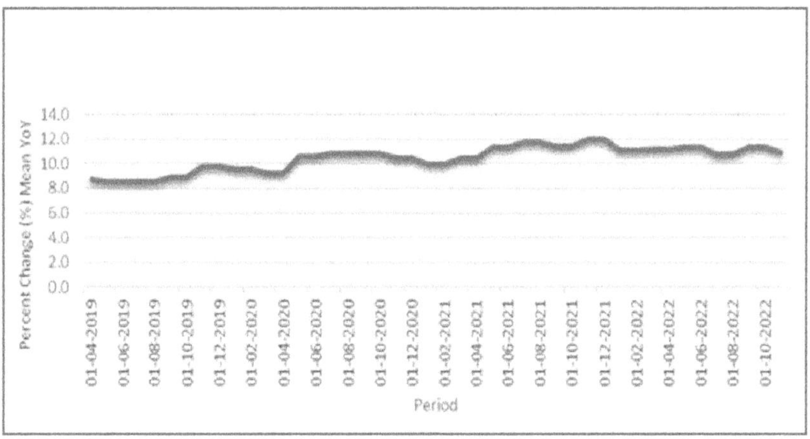

RBI Survey (Household Expectations) 3 Month Forward

Figure 7: Sourced from RBI Surveys Data. Depicting the Household Inflation Expectation, 3-month forward.

The first instance of shock came in September 2020, when the CPI recorded a growth of 7.29 per cent,[43] at a time when the economy was facing a stringent lockdown and consumption was still below optimal. Since then, the CPI has remained above the RBI's comfort zone and is consistently recorded above the upper band of the central bank's target range (2 per cent–4 per cent–6 per cent).[44]

In the first half of FY21 (Q4 FY21), CPI moderated a bit primarily because of a favourable base effect (since CPI is an index, the reading of the previous year plays an important role. Therefore, if the CPI recorded the previous year, same time, was high, then this year's reading will be lower). A similar situation was recorded in Q3 FY21, as base effect was again pacifying the CPI print despite demand recovery in the economy.

Nevertheless, inflationary tendencies were already entrenched in the economy, and the CPI peaked in April 2022 for the period when it was recorded at 7.79 per cent.[45] Unable to anchor the market's inflation expectation (as apparent from the forward household surveys), the RBI began its rate hiking cycle, with the first hike coming into being during the May 2022 policy meeting.

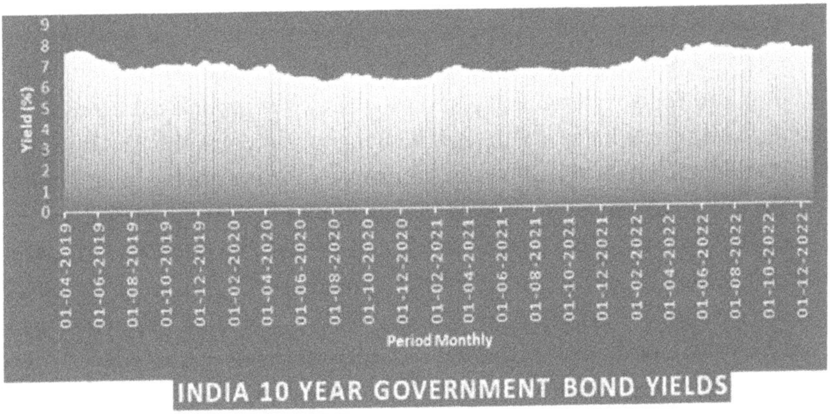

Figure 8: Sourced from RBI, NSDL Data. Depicting the evolution of yields of India 10 year-duration Government debt.

43 Ministry of Statistics and Program Implementation Press Releases | India CPI Data | https://www.mospi.gov.in/web/mospi/press-release1

44 RBI Act | Regulations| https://m.rbi.org.in/scripts/fs_overview.aspx?fn=2752

45 Ministry of Statistics and Program Implementation Press Releases | India CPI Data | https://www.mospi.gov.in/web/mospi/press-release1

Indian government 10-year debt yields, which comprise the largest proportion of its borrowing basket, have increased significantly over the years of the pandemic. Since this category of issued government debt measures the appetite of the market for debt as well as the sustainability of the supply of such debt (from the government), yields of 10-Year Government Security are an important tool in the macroeconomic assessment of India.

Since March 2020, the beginning of the COVID-19 pandemic, the instrument's yields have increased by almost 100 bps, from around 6.5 per cent to 7.55 per cent,[46] recorded in November 2022. The higher the yields, the lower the demand appetite and the higher the anticipated supply of the security instrument. Also, since yields and prices of bonds go in opposite directions, higher yields mean that the price of the security declines. This consequently erodes the value of the investment made by an investor.

In order to compensate the investor for the value erosion, the issuer of such securities must provide a higher coupon rate (or return on the investment), and this increases the interest rate obligation of the Government (which, in this case, is the issuer of the security instrument in the debt market).

Consequently, the Indian government's interest servicing obligation increased by 13 per cent in FY21 and 17 per cent in FY22,[47] despite low interest rates and high systemic liquidity. In FY23, this figure is expected to be higher, or on par with FY22, given the rising interest rate and low liquidity environment, despite robust tax collections by the government.

In FY23, the interest obligations of the government of India were expected to rise by 16 per cent or ₹1.3 lac crore over the previous year's estimate.[48] At ₹9.4 lac crore, interest obligations are the highest seen by Indian administrators. Nevertheless, fiscal deficit has now become a matter of concern for Indian policymakers, and it is estimated to rise just 10 per cent over the previous year to ₹16.6 lac crore (about ₹2 lac crore lower than the deficit in FY21, when the COVID-19 pandemic began).[49]

46 RBI Weekly Statistical Supplement | https://rbi.org.in/Scripts/BS_ViewWSS.aspx
47 India Budget Statistics | https://www.indiabudget.gov.in/
48 India Budget Statistics | https://www.indiabudget.gov.in/
49 India Budget Statistics | https://www.indiabudget.gov.in/

Importantly, as India moves towards a more sustainable fiscal management (as per the Fiscal Responsibility and Budget Management Act, 2003) or FRBM scenario, fiscal deficit is expected to decline in the coming years in order to be under 6 per cent over the next two financial years.

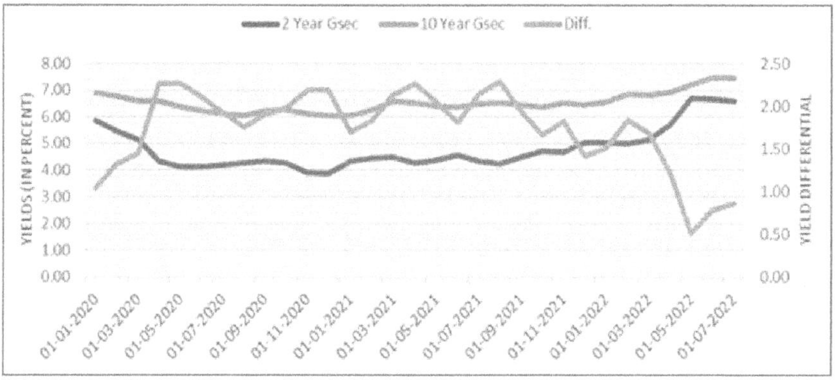

Yield Curve 2 Year & 10 Year Government Securities Movement

Figure 9: Sourced from RBI Data. Depicting the comparison of the yields of India's 2-year and 10-year duration Government debt.

As we ended the FY23, a rising interest rate environment and a somewhat contained government expenditure over the next financial year, the bond market nevertheless emanated turbulence ahead for the Indian economy.

The difference between a 10-year Government Security Yield and a 2-year Government Security Yield, which denotes the health of the economy, was less than 1 per cent in the August-September period of the current financial year.[50] The lower the difference, the higher the risk for the economy stalling, and therefore, this condition augured caution for the Indian economy as it recovered from the pandemic era into a recovery-boom phase.

In 2023, it was expected that the fiscal push would remain in overdrive and fiscal deficit targets would be breached. For the financial year 2022–23, the government had sought parliamentary approval to borrow a net additional $40 billion for capital expenditure, along with food and

50 Author's Estimates based RBI Weekly Data

fertilizer subsidies. This sum was over and above the $487 billion total government expenditure, estimated originally by the annual budget for the year. Consequently, the total government expenditure for the current financial year grew by almost 13 per cent as compared to the previous year and came at a time when the government's tax revenue remained robust.

The RBI, on the other hand, began withdrawing excess liquidity from the system amidst a tightening monetary policy and fired all cylinders to anchor inflation expectations. During a late-year MPC meeting, the central bank raised the benchmark Repo rate by an additional 35 bps and was expected to hike an incremental 25 bps in February, the next year. The market was already anticipating a terminal Repo rate of 6.5 per cent by early 2024, and rate transmission to existing and fresh loans was expected to brutalize the economy.

Until 2023, India, like most of the world, was in what economists define as an 'active fiscal and passive monetary policy' situation. What that meant was that while the government was pushing the boundaries by issuing piles of debt to boost the economy, the RBI was accommodating consumption and investment through low interest rates and liquidity infusion in the system.

With the US Fed becoming hawkish, global capital flows eventually began to shun emerging markets in their flight to safe havens. This route was not only expected to dry out necessary external financing for emerging markets such as India, but also discourages their exports as consumption power is deliberately restricted in the developed world.

To protect the Indian Rupee, the RBI in turn becomes active. Usually, when this happens, the government takes a back seat and focuses on fiscal consolidation by consciously reducing its debt, and this situation is defined by economists as, 'passive fiscal and active monetary policy' situation. However, given the circumstances, the Indian government likely found itself in the most notorious situation, called 'active fiscal and active monetary policies.' This situation is the most difficult as far as economic management is concerned and causes heightened instability in an economy.

Given the background, Indian policymakers must take note of economist, Momi Dahan's renowned 1998 paper, 'Fiscal Effects on Monetary Policy', which discusses the effect of tightening monetary policy on a government's fiscal deficit. Among other suggestions, Dahan shows that in the short term, rising interest rates not only raise the government's fiscal deficit by way of raising interest payment obligations but also impedes its tax revenue amidst fall in output. The need of the hour is to therefore institutionalize a 'Fiscal-Monetary Coordination Committee' that is mandated to meet every quarter to discuss government's expenditure planning and the RBI's reserve and currency operations. This calls for the amendment of the RBI Act's Section 45Y at the earliest. At the same time, policymakers must also realize that the erstwhile approach of institutions working in silos will not work anymore, and that coordination is essential. Time is perhaps ripe to understand that precaution is always better than cure.[51] Answering the policy question, things were managed well, but better nuances are required in effective policy management during crisis times.

51 India's Economic Policy Gridlock can be Solved with Coordination (Nikkie Asia: Karan Mehrishi, 2023) https://asia.nikkei.com/Opinion/India-s-economic-policy-gridlock-can-be-solved-with-coordination

CHAPTER 6

Assessing the Global Response and Impact

Managing Rupee in a Volatile Global Environment

During the peak COVID-19 crisis, given the falling INR and a sense of permanence in inflationary outlook, the RBI carefully weighed its options regarding the three policy goals comprising monetary policy independence, capital flows, and exchange rate management. Perhaps its biggest challenge was the management of the record liquidity created over much of the past two years.

How this liquidity would be unwound amidst rising rates in advanced economies, therefore, decided the next course of Indian central banking. The Indian central bank understood that, like its counterparts elsewhere, if it chose to exert its control over the first policy goal pertaining to an independent monetary policy, raising interest rates would have been the most logical option amidst normalization-led capital outflows and budding inflationary tendencies.

However, such attempts would have automatically raised yields and, in the process, could have made the RBI's balance sheet susceptible to revaluation losses. In line with a recent IMF paper, Asian central banks were stuck in a complex relationship with their governments, disallowing them to conduct their mandates effectively.

In any case, a policy goal prioritizing active exchange rate management, on the other hand, was not new for Asian central banks, as most practised some form of currency supervision. The trick, however, was to identify the level of exchange rate that could be tolerated amidst outflow-led depreciation. Taking lessons from the 1997 Asian financial crisis, RBI therefore had to understand that defending currency beyond a point was actually futile.

This is because, during a crisis, central banks often excessively exhaust their foreign currency reserves to safeguard their currencies and make their balance sheets vulnerable in the process. A potential solution would be an extension of the 'Dollar Liquidity Swap Lines' from the US Fed, instead. Nonetheless, no such policy or arrangement was ever formalized to bring this forward.

The final policy goal pertaining to capital flows management was connected to how well the other two were dealt with at the peak of the COVID-19 pandemic.

It was, therefore, abundantly clear that placing any further controls on foreign capital would have been a waste of time. Given the depreciating Asian currencies (including the INR) and falling yield differentials with the USA-, EU-, Japan-issued debt, there were chances that capital outflows would momentarily destabilize the system. Instead of focusing on strategizing this transition, the recommendation was therefore for the RBI to prepare down its government debt holdings. If conducted, this could have resulted in it raising interest rates that reflected the new market realities and made Indian debt more attractive in the process.

Building buffers, such as increasing investment in Gold, were nevertheless used to defend the balance sheet. Yet, while the RBI decided its next course of action, the central bank dealt with the dilemma pertaining to its mandate to actively manage yields of Government debt, first and foremost.

The Reversal of Quantitative Easing: How it panned out?

The premise on which certain analysts pacified the market was based on their understanding that the USA Fed is magnanimous and that the central bank will rescue the system if push comes to shove. In fact, traders across the world took advantage of a second wind emanating from the belief that the Fed would be careful not to overstep this time and ensconce the market from misfortune. Nevertheless, there was a catch.

Even in the mid-2023, systemic liquidity was nowhere near the lows last seen just before the GFC, the Dot-Com Bubble Burst, or even the Black Monday Crash. Perhaps the best gauge to understand systemic liquidity is through the lens of the time's prevailing M3 levels, as a multiple of base money (M0). Therefore, it can be understood that since 1960, the M3 Multiple in the United States has averaged 10.4.

During 2023, it was 9.0. Towards the build-up to the GFC, the M3 Multiple was averaging 8.6 in the year 2006. Interestingly, the GFC happened despite the Fed's reluctant attempts to restore the systemic liquidity levels to the 9.0+ range in 2007. This was too little, too late, at best. Just before the Dot-Com Bubble Burst in 2000, the M3 Multiple was 7.7 towards the end of 1999. Just before the 1996 ASEAN Financial Crisis, the M3 Multiple was recorded at 8.7!

What this means is that the evergreening crowd simply undermined the USA Fed's determination to squash inflationary tendencies with impunity, and the fact that it would go to any length to meet its objective. Systemic liquidity was still high in 2023, when compared to recent history, and since the Fed deemed inflation a tad bit uncomfortable, global markets remained in permanent turmoil.

For reference: to reach pre-GFC levels of liquidity, the Fed may still withdraw an incremental $1.4 trillion of liquidity from the system. To reach the pre-Dot-Com Bubble Burst levels, it can withdraw an incremental $3 trillion! What happened to the American capital market is one story; the bigger story perhaps pertained to the impending future of the EMs. When $3 trillion worth of yield-chasing capital is withdrawn from the system, things going awry is an understatement.

In 2024, as inflation continues to remain higher than expected, a higher for longer stance is maintained. Still, to maintain a semblance of stability, the Fed Governor continues to provide pacifying commentary by reducing the balance sheet contraction rate to half. Whether this rate of contraction is still high, and what impact it will bring upon the emerging markets, is still nebulous.

Yield Curve Evolution – Looking West Side!

At 360 bps, the USA and India's 10-year GSec (Government Security) yield differential was the lowest in 11 years, sometime in Q4 2022. What that meant was that with the USA Fed raising rates by 75 bps, as on 22nd September 2022, an Indian 10 Government Security was the least attractive since 1st December 2011.

On Average, an Indian 10-year GSec maintained a 545 bps (±68 bps) premium over an equivalent American security during this period. Therefore, in order to achieve that differential, an Indian security should have yielded an incremental 173 bps (as on 23rd September 2022), pegging itself at around 9.12 per cent.

In case critics discounted the yield of 9.12 per cent being too high, the highest yield during the period under consideration was recorded on 19th August 2013, when it was pegged at 9.51 per cent.

Interestingly, the yield differential was 663 bps then.

This happened because of low USA interest rates, but taper tantrums, nonetheless, added incremental interest burden on EM debt instruments, as safe-haven demand (post-GFC) continued to exert downward pressure on US Securities' yields (long end of the curve).

This time, however, actual monetary tightening occurred at a frightening pace, and it is possible that EM volatility would have resulted in an even higher demand for USA long-duration government securities. As certain small economies collapse, this pace received a fillip. Additionally, given the over 8 per cent USA Inflation during much of 2022, either yields should have risen further or inflation should have come down, for returns to become positive.

In the prevalent scenario, the former condition looked more realistic, putting looming pressure on Indian & other EM debt. At the least, considering the lower end of the StD, Indian 10-year GSec yields should have touched 8.4 per cent in the months that followed, as the Fed showed some more of its ruthless side. Forward markets were, nevertheless, expecting the yields to be around 7.45 per cent (1 year forward), primarily because of yield curve flattening and improving tax buoyancy. It was nevertheless not clear whether history or forward guidance would win the race.

In Q2 2024, we were yet again facing a similar situation, as the USA's interest rates are expected to remain higher for longer, putting pressure on EM debt. Accompanied yields are serious macro considerations now, and since EMs may be forced to lower rates faster than the developed world, we may see a similar situation panning out.

State of Global Monetary Policy: The Rates & Growth Dilemma

The biggest question confronting most central bank watchers was, quite frankly, 'will they, won't they?' Irrespective of whether it pertained to the US Federal Reserve, the ECB, or the RBI.

Apart from prevarications, perhaps the most important pillar of this ambiguity was the central banks' inability to determine the inflation trajectory, so much so that 'transitory' became a dirty word. The question that everyone asked was whether central bankers themselves could realistically gauge inflation in a dynamically unstable equilibria between inflation and real interest rates (along with unemployment as an external independent variable)?

As a reference, Thomas Piketty, the famous French economist, associated the reason for global wealth inequality to the simple economic function of 'R>G'. In other words, he contends that historically, the rate of growth has been lower than the rate of returns and therefore, the capital owner has become/will become wealthy irrespective of the rate of economic expansion. Monetary economists Roger Farmer and Pawel Zabczyk used an overlapping generation model to prove their interpretation of the 'Fiscal Theory of Price Level' and have shown startling results on why inflation estimation is so tedious during times like these for any central banker.

According to this model, a steady state equilibrium is said to be dynamically efficient when 'interest rate is greater than the rate of growth'. Contrary to the contention of those economists who believe that high growth can solve the current problems faced by the global economy, it is stated that, when interest rates are lower than economic growth, then the steady state becomes dynamically inefficient!

So, high growth might actually complicate things further? Why this finding is such a big deal in today's context is that a dynamically inefficient steady state equilibrium is 'associated with indeterminacy'. Therefore, for a realistic estimation of price level and the discount factor, when monetary policy becomes hawkish, governments must become passive, which is not the case. When both fiscal and monetary authorities are all guns blazing and neither is willing to take a back seat, it is therefore impossible to figure out the relationship of 'inflation & real interest rates' with the 'actual state of the economy'. In other words, there is no way central bankers (or, for that matter, specialist monetary economists) can realistically figure out the inflation trajectory from the state of the economy alone, no matter which macro models they use. What this means is that along with our 'omnipotent' central banks, we are staring at the abyss, and none of us knows what the future holds. As governments continued to rely on deficit financing, while monetary authorities tightened, the inflation trajectory for much of 2023 transformed itself into the world's most dangerous roller-coaster ride.

CHAPTER 7

An Assessment of Global Central Bank Balance Sheets

The COVID-19 pandemic which is being termed as a Black Swan event in this book forced the global institutional framework to rethink its tried and tested strategies.

History teaches us that the chances of dealing with such an eventuality are one in a million!

The fact of the matter is that no one could have ever anticipated an event of this magnitude, and the world was ill-prepared for such an economic and the associated humanitarian catastrophe.

In the first instance, however, the world's capacity to contain this pandemic appeared easier said than done. Given humanity's collective achievements in the fields of medicine, governance, management, and technology, there was a sense of confidence among policymakers that things could be managed well in time.

Still, it came as a rude shock that things went out of hand, not because the world did not have the ability or the resources, but rather, lacked initial synergy. Truth be told, while it is true that the global economy is today more integrated than ever, it is also important to understand that it operates within a complex mesh of fundamental variables, which are in a constant state of flux. Concepts of reserve currencies, trade blocs, political ideologies, and developmental priorities are, therefore, realities that one cannot ignore.

What this means is that while we live in a globalized economy, there are stark differences among nations, and their socio-economic realities determine their relations with each other. This percolates in the way each country's domestic institutional framework operates and eventually interacts with the global framework. It can therefore be argued that the single biggest problem in effectively managing the pandemic was the world's failure to put up a united front, despite the so-called behemoth unilateral institutions, such as the World Bank, the IMF, the Bank of International Settlements (BIS), and the ADB acting as global binders. Even before the COVID-19 pandemic arrived, protectionism was rising across the world, and important economic powers of the world were largely ruled by right-leaning governments.

At the same time, some nations were, and still are, ruled by dictators with left-leaning ideologies.

This, in combination with an unprecedented shock, forced local institutional frameworks of every country to reassess and rework their strategies. The resultant spill over to the global institutions then was just a function of time, and soon the management of a localized epidemic became a full-fledged pandemic operation. In other words, COVID-19 merely uncovered what was hidden.

This chapter is thus dedicated to the assessment of how local institutional frameworks functioned and evolved during the crises, with local realities in the background. I believe that the balance sheets of major central banks across the world give us a grounding in these local impact assessments, and the later global spill-overs.

In this chapter, we will try to understand the local realities of four central banks and how they influenced each other. Local-to-global institutional interaction is therefore the primary concern here.

Consequently, the assessment limits itself to the balance sheets of four central banks, namely:

1. The US Federal Reserve System (Fed)
2. The European Central Bank (ECB)
3. The Bank of Japan (BOJ)
4. The Reserve Bank of India (RBI)

Initially, I believe that a comprehensive understanding can be undertaken by studying the composition transformations of central bank balance sheets.

The following analysis concerns itself solely with this aspect:

Structural & Composition Transformations of Balance Sheets

There is a famous remark by former Treasury Secretary, John Connoly, which goes like this,

> The Dollar is our currency, but your problem!

So, when we talk about local spillovers having international repercussions, perhaps a discussion on the status of the USD and the actions of the US Federal Reserve System is paramount.

Just an example to set the tone here. By way of direct purchase of securities over a period of nearly 72 months, the quantum of liquidity created by the US Federal Reserve during the Global Financial Crisis (GFC) was roughly $3.7 trillion. While this number is $4.2 trillion in response to the COVID-19 crisis, what's surprising is the rate of deployment, as this liquidity was created in just under 16 months. The story is similar when one considers the liquidity created by the ECB, BOJ, and the Bank of England during this period.

Table 12: US Federal Reserve (US Fed) Balance Sheet Assessment. Sourced from Federal Reserve data and author calculations.

	Balance Sheet Size (USD Tn)	Growth	CIC* (USD Tn)	Growth	Securities Held (USD Tn)	Growth
1st Jan 2020	4.15		1.81		3.76	
1st June 2020	7.16	73%	1.95	8%	5.97	59%
11th April 2021	7.79	9%	2.16	11%	7.24	21%
11th April 2022	8.96	15%	2.27	5%	8.51	18%
11th April 2023	8.61	−4%	2.32	2%	7.88	−7%
11th April 2024	7.41	−14%	2.35	1%	6.93	−12%

*Note: Federal Reserve System Board Data; *CIC: Currency in Circulation*

By June 2020, the US Federal Reserve increased its balance sheet size to an unprecedented $7.2 trillion (from ~$4.2 trillion, six months earlier), growing by over 73 per cent in the period. This exercise created significant liquidity not only in the US economy but also globally, simply because of the reserve currency status of the USD, and the fact that the country is a major consumerist force in the world.

If one assesses the actions taken by the Federal Reserve, then it is important to look at the modulation of the asset side, where securities held increased to almost $6 trillion by June 2020.

This unleashed significant liquidity, as represented by institutional deposits, and credit offtake rose consequently to unprecedented levels. This, in a way, had repercussions similar to those seen in 2008–09, during the Great Financial Crisis (GFC).

Resultantly, US capital market valuations surged, and fixed income yields plummeted. Significant liquidity, on the back of almost zero interest rate policy (ZIRP), also turned into what is popularly known as 'yield chasing capital', and shored up the valuations of emerging markets, offering higher returns.

This, in turn, offered American investors two benefits: one, of course, higher comparative yields/returns, and the other being a function of inflow of foreign capital. This 'carry' offered an arbitrage opportunity to investors and traders alike, given the appreciation of the local currency of the investee markets.

As far as the Effective Fund Rate was concerned, by the middle of April 2021, rates were pegged at 0.07 per cent – a sharp decline from the 1.55 per cent seen at the beginning of the crisis.

Table 13. The Fed's LM During the Crisis.

	Institutional Deposits (USD Tn)	Temporal Liquidity Creation (USD Tn)	Effective Fund Rate
1st Jan 2020	1.68		1.55%
1st June 2020	3.26	1.58	0.08%
11th April 2021	3.95	0.69	0.07%
11th April 2022	3.79	−0.16	0.33%
11th April 2023	3.35	−0.44	4.83%
11th April 2024	3.34	−0.01	5.33%

Sourced from Federal Reserve data and author calculations.

Temporal liquidity in the six-month period, until June 2020, increased by almost $1.6 trillion, and further by $0.7 trillion, over the next 10 months. The corresponding doubling of institutional deposits was again unprecedented, with commercial banks flush with cash.

The accommodation (both fiscal and monetary) increased household consumption power as well, allowing for demand stability and investor confidence.

While inflation remained an important consideration, given the combination of capacity destruction (on the back of the COVID pandemic), as well as geopolitical tensions, household confidence remained resilient in the US economy, with unemployment numbers remaining low.

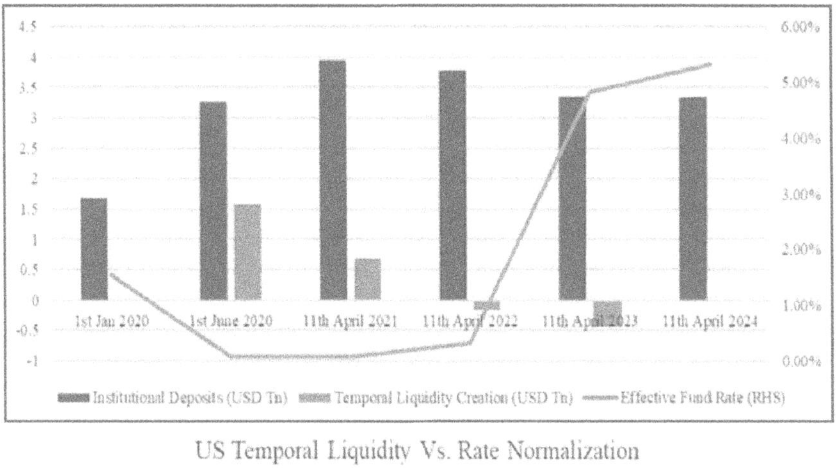

Figure 10: Depicting the US Temporal Liquidity evolution (compared to rates) during the COVID period.

Sourced from the Federal Reserve System Board. Chart: Karan Mehrishi.

These strong economic conditions in the United States resulted in imported inflationary conditions for other countries, which were reeling under economic stresses. American yield chasing capital also appreciated currencies of major emerging markets (on the back of inflows), giving a semblance of resilience, but ultimately feeding into a higher import bill and deteriorating balance of payment scenarios.

By April 2023, however, interest rates normalized significantly on the back of a strong economy, accompanied by rising core inflation. The Federal Reserve responded by contracting its balance sheet and providing a timeline of liquidity absorption, spooking not only the USA's institutional framework but also the global financial architecture. The event described by the maxim, 'Taper Tantrums', had finally begun.

Table 14: European Central Bank (ECB) Balance Sheet Assessment. Sourced from ECB data and author calculations.

	Balance Sheet (Euro Tn)	Growth	CIC* (Euro Tn)	Growth	Securities Held (Euro Tn)	Growth
Dec 19	4.67		1.29		2.85	
Dec 20	6.97	49%	1.43	14%	3.89	36%
Dec 21	8.56	23%	1.54	11%	4.89	26%
Dec 22	7.95	−7%	1.57	3%	5.11	4%
Dec 23	6.89	−13%	1.56	−1%	4.91	−4%

*Note: European Central Bank/Euro System Data; *CIC: Currency in Circulation*

In many ways, the balance sheet of the ECB shares a lot of similarities with that of the US Federal Reserve.

This has happened probably because the United States and the European Union represent what is popularly called the West, which, in turn, is synonymous with the rich world. What that means is that the balance sheets represent the socio-economic realities of two very similar regions, with little disparity.

Consequently, if one looks at the overall balance sheet dynamics here, it is clear that components are in a way intertwined. While the size of the overall balance sheets of both central banks increased rapidly in 2020, from roughly the same size, the temporal liquidity also moved in tandem.

Moreover, interest rates modulation also seemed to be well-coordinated, with interest rates only normalizing in mid-2021 – even though the US Fed preceded the ECB by about three months.

Until the end of 2020, however, a low-interest rate environment in the European Union became an accepted phenomenon and slowly abetted the fires of inflation. While the Euro Area did not witness a rising trend until March 2021, there were indeed pressures emanating from consumer demand.

The trouble for both the EU and the US economies was the fact that fiscal incentivization allowed households to sit on a lot of cheap money (popularly known as Helicopter Money in Economics), enticing them to consume.

Deficit financing, just like everywhere else in the world, also became a norm in the name of public good, and the ECB obliged by gobbling up unprecedented amounts of Government debt during this time. CIC, as a result, grew by over 12 per cent during much of 2020 and 2021.

However, the COVID pandemic had negative repercussions on global supply chains, and demand pressures led to inflationary tendencies across the world. Such were the cost pressures that the Euro Area inflation number stood at 5 per cent in December 2021, a full 530 bps higher than the same time the previous year.

With the ECB maintaining interest rates at 0 per cent, inflation continued its upward trajectory, finally settling at 10.6 per cent in October 2022. This was also a time when the supply of Russian Oil declined to the EU, plummeting the region into significant economic hardships.

In the backdrop of the Russian invasion of Ukraine, the European Union had made a conscious decision to reduce its dependence on Russian Oil, which was, until then, the backbone of the European industrial capacities. Households were also dependent on Russian Gas for heating, and the impact was especially felt during the peak of the winter months.

The ECB had to, however, intervene with an increase in rates to 2.5 per cent. While this was expected given the mounting inflation numbers (both core and headline), the preceding taper tantrums were making the markets nervous, as the US Fed was anyway on a tightening schedule.

With a contracting balance sheet size of below 4 trillion Euros, temporal liquidity was in a deficit of 300 billion Euros towards the end of 2022. A new era of normalization had begun, and both the ECB and the Euro Area Fiscal Authorities are finding themselves in a defensive mode (as of mid-2024), as they coordinate to identify the ideal, yet elusive, inflation-growth trade-off.

Table 15: The ECB's LM During the Crisis. Sourced from ECB data and author calculations.

	Institutional Deposits (Euro Tn)	Temporal Liquidity Creation (Euro Tn)	Effective Rate (RHS)
Dec 19	1.81		0%
Dec 20	3.49	1.68	0%
Dec 21	4.29	0.8	0%
Dec 22	3.99	−0.3	2.5%
Dec 23	3.51	−0.48	4.5%

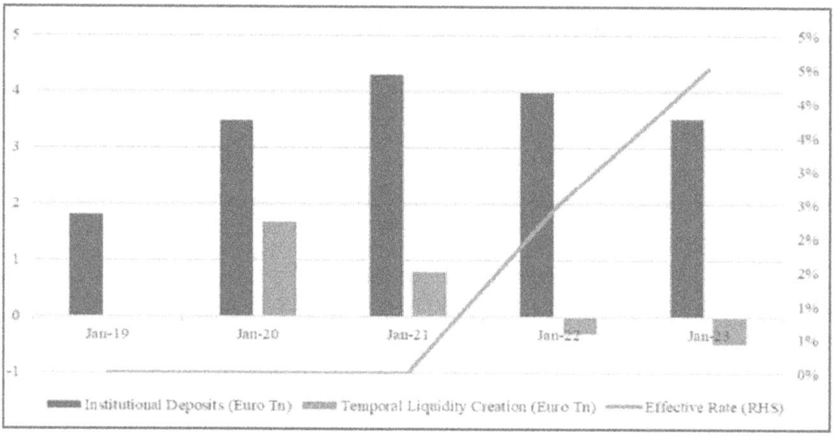

Euro Area Temporal Liquidity Vs. Rate Normalization

Figure 11: Depicting the Euro System Temporal Liquidity evolution (compared to rates) during the COVID period.

Sourced from European Central Bank/Euro System Data. Chart: Karan Mehrishi.

BOJ Balance Sheet Assessment

The BOJ traditionally carries a very large and diversified balance sheet, and is often described as the key market mover. Given the diversity of its balance sheet, with various corporate debt instruments (including those of ETFs), as well as corporate stocks finding themselves on the asset side, BOJ is a force to reckon with, and by virtue decides the direction the Japanese capital markets take.

Therefore, clearly, interest rate modulations, as well as currency interventions, are not the only monetary instruments used by the central bank.

Going one step further, the BOJ has become agnostic to the type of instrument it trades, and leverages its entire balance sheet to stabilize the market. By this virtue, the BOJ's balance sheet has also evolved into the single largest driver of Japanese secondary markets, and security tradability is no longer limited to Government Securities (GSecs).

During COVID-19 pandemic, the BOJ continued to evolve its balance sheet to absorb the shock on the Japanese economy to the greatest extent, while also performing its function as a key fiscal financier.

Table 16: The BoJ's Balance Sheet Assessment. Sourced from BOJ data and author calculations.

	Balance Sheet Yen ('000)	Growth	CIC* Yen ('000)	Growth	Securities Held Yen ('000)	Growth
June 30 2019	5,64,86,65,00,562		1,07,69,27,91,073		516063293993	
Jan 30 2020	5,78,33,52,26,757	2.4%	1,08,96,88,15,619	1.2%	528191820313	2.4%
June 30 2020	6,48,94,62,47,903	12.2%	1,13,27,79,63,336	4.0%	575329834012	8.9%
June 30 2021	7,16,90,06,30,032	10.5%	1,16,59,26,90,261	2.9%	585327281325	1.7%
June 30 2022	7,32,73,06,70,017	2.2%	1,20,18,62,80,596	3.1%	599941066565	2.5%
June 30 2023	7,32,82,85,86,507	0.0%	1,21,37,84,23,185	1.0%	639894327485	6.7%
June 30 2024	7,53,67,09,69,498	2.8%	1,18,90,98,03,367	−2.0%	634360323758	−0.9%

*Note: Bank of Japan (BOJ) Data; *CIC: Currency in Circulation*

The trouble, however, was that the BOJ balance sheet was expanded, while the Japanese economy contracted, year on year. While the phenomenon was experienced by other global central banks as well, the difference was that the Japanese economy continued its downward spiral even in the calendar years following 2020.

With a perennial Negative Interest Rate Policy (NIRP), BOJ continued to remain extremely accommodative; nevertheless, its balance sheet has become unsustainably large.

As an example, to explain the anomaly here, the BOJ's balance sheet was roughly ~79 per cent of the Japanese GDP in mid-2020. Today (as of mid-2024), it has attained the size equivalent of over ~120 per cent of the Japanese GDP.

Building up inflationary tendencies was just a matter of time, and a combination of fiscal and monetary accommodations provided the fodder to investment and consumption functions to grow.

Even though the consumption function is of lesser significance for Japan in the context of falling birth rates, the rising dependents-to-working-group ratio has had negative repercussions on the economy, nevertheless.

The investment function, however, took on a massive proportion thanks to cheap Japanese capital providing an arbitrage opportunity to investors, both domestic and global.

Astoundingly, the BOJ's balance sheet expanded by over 10 per cent between June 2020 and 2021, while the economy contracted.

Table 17: The BoJ's LM During the Crisis. Sourced from BOJ data and author calculations.

	Institutional Deposits Yen ('000)	Temporal Deposits Yen ('000)	Interest Rate
30th June 2019	4,10,64,42,19,088		−0.10%
30th January 2020	4,03,28,97,66,671	−7354452417	−0.10%
30th June 2020	4,47,01,96,29,229	43729862558	−0.10%
30th June 2021	5,37,91,05,75,450	90890946221	−0.10%
30th June 2022	5,52,30,49,32,523	14394357073	−0.10%
30th June 2023	5,44,44,47,67,754	−7860164769	−0.10%
30th June 2024	5,51,77,14,45,604	7326677850	0.10%

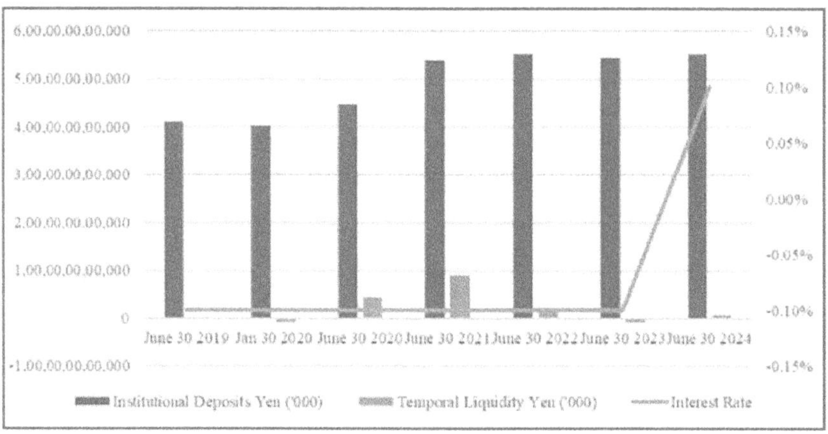

Bank of Japan Temporal Liquidity Vs. Interest Rates

Figure 12: Depicting the BOJ Temporal Liquidity evolution (compared to rates) during the COVID period.

Sourced from Bank of Japan (BOJ) data. Chart: Karan Mehrishi.

CIC during the process expanded by nearly 2 per cent on average, and this can be considered a fuel for the broad money, in turn fuelling system liquidity.

Credit disbursement as a result was extensive, and Japanese capital maintains its 'yield chasing capital' status, on the lines of its counterparts, the USD, and the Euro.

During taper tantrums and the normalization process of the US Fed, the USD began its ascent, and the Japanese Yen soon became the worst-performing currency in the developed world. This was mitigated to an extent by the BOJ via its own balance sheet, but

Institutional deposits declined in the first half of the calendar year 2023, and consequently so did the temporal liquidity. Nevertheless, the BOJ balance sheet has never really contracted until this day, and is ready to take on any eventuality that might need its attention, whether it emanates from commercial banking or the capital market.

Normalization that happened in the first half of 2024 was an event in itself, given the fact that the BOJ exited the Negative Interest Rate Policy (NIRP) for the first time in eight years. A new era of Japanese central banking has truly arrived.

Table 18: RBI Balance Sheet Assessment.

	Balance Sheet (INR Cr.)	Growth	CIC* (INR Cr.)	Growth	Securities Held (NDA)	Growth
FY19	4102905		21,68,797		9,89,877	
FY20	5334792	30.0%	26,35,575	21.5%	11,72,027	18.4%
FY21	5707669	7.0%	28,26,862	7.3%	13,33,173	13.7%
FY22	6190302	8.5%	31,05,720	9.9%	14,88,815	11.7%
FY23	6344756	2.5%	33,48,244	7.8%	14,06,422	−5.5%
FY24	7047703	11.1%	34,78,039	3.9%	13,63,368	−3.1%

Sourced from RBI data and author calculations.

*Note: RBI Data; *CIC: Currency in Circulation*

A lot has been talked about the motions of the RBI balance sheet in the previous pages, but for the sake of this chapter, one can discuss the perspectives of a central bank in a developing/emerging country.

It is important to note that in the current context, the RBI is the only central bank that does not belong in the category, that is represented by the above category. The US Fed, the ECB, as well as the BOJ represent the advanced nations, and anchor the capital markets of the world's foremost nodes of capital.

Therefore, again in the current context, the central banks discussed in precedence are powerful institutions by way of their ability to modulate global capital movements. The RBI, on the other hand, represents a capital recipient economy, and by virtue can be considered to be a 'back-stopper' central bank.

By this virtue, the balance sheet of the RBI operates differently from those operated by advanced economies, and the modulation of Net Foreign Asset (NFA) and NDA, within the Reserve Money (RM) becomes paramount.

This is because an increase in inflows of foreign capital increases the NFA, and a reduction reduced the account. In the latter situation, the NDA (which comprises domestic Government securities) is then utilized to compensate the asset side RM.

Additionally, the NFA is used 100 per cent to backstop CIC by the RBI, and this makes the category an extremely important component of the RBI's balance sheet.

Therefore, it can be understood that the RBI's balance sheet's anchor is foreign asset holdings, and not domestic. The argument is separate from the RBI's function as a banker to the Government of India, as the former deals with its banking and currency safeguarding operations.

What this means is that the RBI controls the sanctity of its balance sheet with the exclusive use of Indian Government securities, and foreign assets, including Gold (for banking operations), and foreign assets, including Gold (for issuer operations).

Resultantly, unlike the central banks discussed earlier, the RBI does not leverage its balance sheet to safeguard the system by giving space to private, non-government debt/stocks.

This is perhaps the fundamental difference between the balance sheets of the big three and those of the RBI. During the COVID pandemic, this character was witnessed in all its glory.

While the era of quantitative easing (QE) flooded the RBI's balance sheet with foreign assets (given the advent of cheap, yield-chasing foreign capital, absorbed via open market, banking operations), the era of its reversal (following taper tantrums) resulted in recedence.

Moreover, during the balance sheet normalizations and interest rate modulations among the big three, the RBI was forced to protect its currency's value (in this case, the INR) by selling major portions of its foreign assets (especially USD reserves) in the open market (both forward and spot).

This resulted in significant stress on the RBI's balance sheet, and a scramble for Gold, and USD became a constant in the central bank's asset management policy. Coming back to the main business of this chapter, the RBI's balance sheet expanded by 30 per cent in the COVID year, thanks to significant fiscal resource mobilization, and resulted in liquidity creation in the system.

In an out-of-turn MPC meeting, the RBI reduced the Repo rate by 75 bps, to 4.4 per cent. This was the signalling of its intent to protect the economy from the burden of uncertainty, and more was yet to come.

Significant temporal liquidity was created with rate cuts that followed, and this eventually allowed banks to expand credit disbursements significantly. One of the offshoots of this exercise was the unsustainable growth recorded by personal loans (non-collateralized loan categories), recording average expansion rates in the vicinity of 20–22 per cent. Overall credit offtake recorded a consistent growth, soon outstripping deposit growth. While this allowed commercial banks to record robust net interest margins (NIM) and a consistent Return on Assets of around 1 per cent, the credit to deposit ratio emanated signs of weakness. Nevertheless, the increased credit offtake resulted in a glut in the CRR category on the RBI's balance sheet, and this was in line with sustained liquidity creation in the system.

Geopolitical disputes elsewhere in the world, combined with a slowdown in Chinese manufacturing output, as well as uneven monsoon (impacting domestic food output), resulted in inflation tendencies building up across the economy.

Consequently, abatement occurred in the second half of the financial year 2023, when normalization finally took out systemic liquidity, and a scramble at the MSF was witnessed, from smaller commercial banks.

As of this date, the RBI is busy building up buffers on the asset side to fight an imminent battle with safe havens outflows, and the triggering balance sheet normalizations of the big three central banks.

While inflation may have abated in the medium term, a full-blown financial crisis is a nemesis of all central banks listed here. The expectation of a soft landing is perhaps the only saviour.

Table 19: The RBI's LM During the Crisis.

	Deposits (INR Cr.)	Temporal Liquidity (INR Cr.)	Repo Rate
FY19	7,64,922		6%
FY20	11,75,860	4,10,938	4.40%
FY21	14,91,537	3,15,677	4%
FY22	17,33,787	2,42,250	4.40%
FY23	13,54,217	−3,79,570	6.50%
FY24	17,19,838	3,65,621	6.50%

Sourced from RBI data and author calculations.

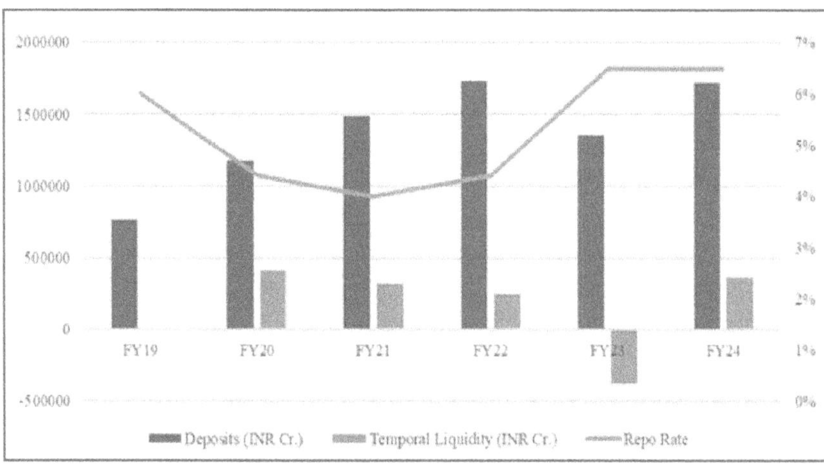

RBI Temporal Liquidity Vs. Interest Rates

Figure 13: Depicting the RBI Temporal Liquidity evolution (compared to rates) during the COVID period.

Source from RBI Data. Chart: Karan Mehrishi.

Comparing the balance sheets of the above-discussed central banks vis-à-vis the RBI, it is noted that the latter expanded its balance sheet by 12 per cent on average (over the discussed four-year period, i.e., 2020–2023). This makes the RBI's balance sheet expansion being third largest among the discussed four central banks. While the components of the balance sheet differ, given the differences in securities (type and category) held, the RBI security holdings increased on average by 10 per cent, as compared to the US Fed and ECB, seeing expansions of 23 per cent and 16 per cent, respectively. This suggests that the Indian central bank created sufficient collateralized space and managed the collateral constraint problem well. This, in turn, also means that sufficient liquidity support was provided to the system by the RBI, as compared to other major central banks of the developed world.

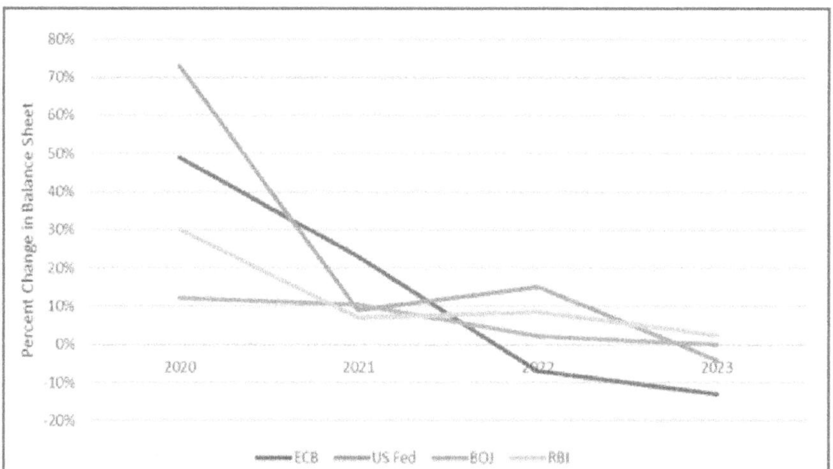

Balance Sheet Evolution of Major Central Banks

Figure 14: Depicting Central Bank Balance Sheet evolution during the COVID period. *Sourced from major central bank annual reports. Chart: Karan Mehrishi.*

US Fed Liquidity Swap Arrangement: A Brief Discussion

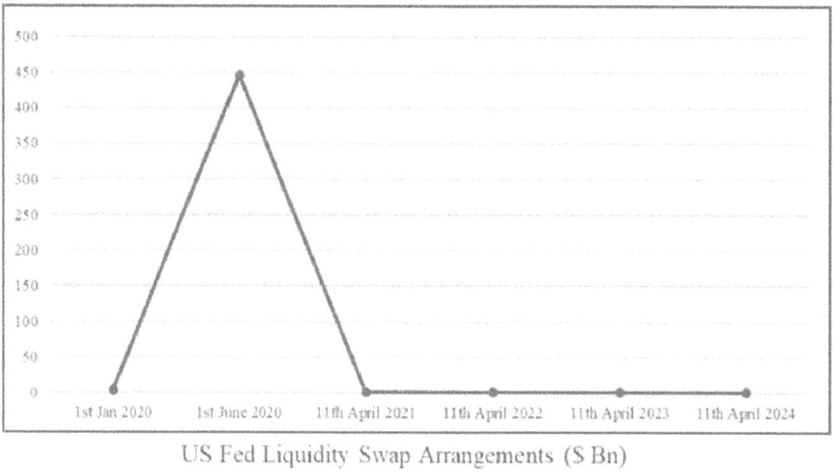

Figure 15: Depicting the utilization of the Swap Lines during the COVID period.
Sourced from US Federal Reserve Data. Chart: Karan Mehrishi.

Under the authority of the Federal Reserve Act (Section 14), the US Federal Reserve had established the Dollar Swap Lines with fourteen central banks across the world.

These central banks, which include systemically important banks such as the BOJ, the ECB, the Bank of England, the Bank of Canada, and the Swiss Central Bank, among others, are entitled to borrow USD at spot rates during crisis periods.

The purpose of this instrument is to provide access to cheap USD to core economies of the world, during a crisis, when the value of the USD soars (on safe-haven demand), and domestic financial institutions and businesses find it difficult to meet their USD obligations sustainably.

The repayment of the borrowed USD is determined to be at a pre-decided spot rate (irrespective of the prevailing exchange rates), at a mutually agreed-upon date. Consequently, the arrangement's purpose is to minimize crises related stresses, and to afford flexibility to the borrowing nation's financial system.

The constitution of these Swap Lines was a function of the contagion of the GFC, which was fast spreading to other nations/ regions, having close ties with the US capital market.

At the peak of the GFC (the first week of December 2008), the Dollar Swap Lines arranged for a transmission of over $583 billion to associated/ covered central banks from the US Federal Reserve System.

While the facility sees minimal activity for most of the period, post the GFC, another spike in the arrangement's utilization came in early 2012, when over $100 billion was transmitted to the global system.

During the peak of the COVID-19-triggered financial crisis (May 2020), the facility saw the flow of over $450 billion to associated central banks, providing significant comfort to their respective financial systems.

While the idea is that some of the USD made available to the 'major' central banks would then percolate to other central banks in the respective regions as well, there is little proof that this ever happens.

Major emerging market central banks such as the RBI and the ASEAN region are not part of the arrangement, and are therefore invariably forced to fend for themselves in times of crises or USD safe-haven demand-related outflows.

This is a subject that remains contentious, and perhaps the most important topic of discussion in global central banking.

The COVID crisis, just like other financial crises before it, has exposed the lack of coordination among central banks and their biased LM approaches during unfavourable events.

CHAPTER 8

Recommendations & Learnings

Reimagining the Policy Implementation Framework of the RBI[52]

The RBI has been consistently narrowing its monetary corridor (**see Note 1**) ever since its introduction in 2011. Consequently, the system generally remains in ex ante liquidity deficit, which is part of a broader strategy[53] to have more control over systemic LM via better alignment of the Weighted Average Overnight Call Money Rate (WACR) with the prevailing Repo rate.[54] This stance is achieved by consistent liquidity absorptions via multiple conventional and unconventional monetary policy tools, perhaps even more so after the adoption of the Flexible Inflation Targeting Regime[55] in 2016. While this has helped the RBI in managing its price stability mandate,[56] the central bank has been unable to manage[57] the volatility in the non-collateralized inter-bank fund

52 This is the author's original research, and part of his submitted coursework at Yale University.

53 Banking Development and Perspectives "Reliance on Call Money Market Component" (RBI, 2002) https://www.rbi.org.in/scripts/PublicationsView.aspx?Id=4555

54 Minutes of the Federal Open Market Committee "Exit Strategy Principals Component" (Federal Reserve Board) https://www.federalreserve.gov/monetarypolicy/fomcminutes20110622.htm

55 Inflation Targeting in India: An Interim Assessment (World Bank Group: Barry Eichengreen et al., 2021) https://openknowledge.worldbank.org/server/api/core/bitstreams/bfd1f553-0baf-5e3e-8644-86ae90be697b/content

56 Liquidity Crisis Threatens RBI's Economic Growth Push (Policy Circle, 2025) https://www.policycircle.org/economy/liquidity-crisis-threatens-economy/

57 Liquidity Management and Monetary Transmission: Empirical Analysis for India (Emerald: Charmal et al., 2022) https://www.emerald.com/insight/content/doi/10.1108/jes-07-2020-0359/full/html

market (**see Note 2**) to the detriment[58] of smaller commercial banks.[59] This volatility is caused by a lack of liquidity uniformity in the system (emphasised since the COVID phase), which is the result of a situation where large commercial banks hoard excess reserves, taking advantage of a condition called 'heterogenous distribution of liquidity',[60] influencing WACR spreads, vis-à-vis the policy rate. The section is therefore an attempt to imagine a reformed monitory corridor that is in line with the current market realities, and has enough flexibility built into it to adapt to changing conditions.

The WACR was introduced as an 'operating target rate' after a thorough review of India's Monetary Policy Framework in July 2011.[61] The WACR was to be aligned with the prevailing fixed rate Repo rate, and was supposed to move within a monetary corridor with two thresholds – the MSF being the upper bound, and the fixed rate Reverse Repo rate being the lower. The Repo rate, on the other hand, is at the centre of the corridor. Collectively, this corridor became part of the LAF, which was a monetary tool to control systemic liquidity,[62] while ensuring financial stability. Accordingly, the WACR became the RBI's official 'liquidity targeting tool'. In order to maintain efficiency and have a well-understood operating procedure, the RBI imposed a 200 bps fixed differential between the upper and the lower bound, with the Repo rate being 100 bps equidistant to both the thresholds. Meanwhile, Variable Reverse Repo/ Repo operations are utilized to sanitize the system, as part of the mandate to align WACR and Repo rate. Before the implementation of

58 Issues on Liquidity Management in Banking System: An Empirical Evidence from Indian Commercial Banks (Cogent Economics & Finance: Sharma et al., 2022) https://www.tandfonline.com/doi/full/10.1080/23322039.2022.2122190#abstract

59 Liquidity Easing to Moderate Indian Banks' NIMs Pressure as Rates Fall (Fitch Rating, 2025) https://www.fitchratings.com/research/banks/liquidity-easing-to-moderate-indian-banks-nim-pressure-as-rates-fall-12-02-2025#:~:text=System%20liquidity%20pressures%20have%20moderated,a%20key%20factor%20to%20watch.

60 Drivers of WACR-Repo Rate Spread: An Empirical Analysis of India (Kalsie et al., 2023) https://journals.sagepub.com/doi/10.1177/09721509231166257

61 RBI Monetary Policy Statement: Governor Dr. Subbarao (RBI, 2011–12) https://www.voiceofca.in/siteadmin/document/RBI_Monetary_Policy_Statement_for_2011-12_Press_Statement.pdf

62 Corridors and Floors of Monetary Policy (Liberty Street Economics: Todd Keister, 2012) https://libertystreeteconomics.newyorkfed.org/2012/04/corridors-and-floors-in-monetary-policy/

the regime, the fixed rate Repo, and Reverse Repo rate differential ranged between 100 to 300 bps (between years 2000 and 2011), with virtually no other collateralized window existing. After 2011 reforms, the MSF has become the most expensive source of funding for banks and can be accessed by dipping up to 3 per cent of the Statutory Liquidity Ratio (SLR) portfolio **(see Note 7)**, which in turn comprises government securities and cash, and is currently fixed at 18 per cent of NDTL. The SLR is a regulatory requirement and is mandatory for all commercial banks. The monetary corridor was, however, further finetuned in 2016, when the Urjit Patel Expert Panel[63] recommended the narrowing of the corridor to 100 bps, from the previous 200 bps. With this change, the Repo rate was 50 bps equidistant to both MSF and the fixed rate Reverse Repo Rate. Nevertheless, the RBI's April 2017 Statement on Development and Regulatory Policies recommended a further narrowing of the corridor to 50 bps, resulting in the Repo rate being just 25 bps equidistant to both the MSF and fixed rate Reverse Repo rate. The RBI justified this narrowing by stating that it was essential 'to ensure the fine alignment of the WACR, that is the operating target of its monetary policy with the prevailing policy rate, that is the Repo rate'.[64] The idea was to have 'a narrower corridor in order to be more effective in managing overnight liquidity situations, when participants accumulate on one side of the market', resulting in financial stresses and slowing of the transmission process (of policy actions). This was done in the aftermath of the Demonetization exercise of 2016, when the Indian Government forced the RBI to demonetize over 90 per cent of all CIC, and which resulted in high systemic LM problems due to excessive deposit growth. The strategy was tested yet again when the RBI faced problems during the COVID-19 crisis, when deposit growth again outstripped credit growth, flushing commercial banks with excess reserves.[65] This event resulted in commercial banks scrambling to park these reserves with the RBI

63 Report of Expert Committee to Revise and Strengthen the Monetary Policy Framework (RBI, 2014) https://rbidocs.rbi.org.in/rdocs/PublicationReport/Pdfs/ECOMRF210114_F.pdf

64 Statement on Developmental and Regulatory Polies (RBI, 2017) https://www.rbi.org.in/commonman/english/scripts/PressReleases.aspx?Id=2219

65 RBI's Post Covid Monetary and Liquidity Measures: Impact on Money, Bond, and Credit Markets (NIBM: Jiji T Mathew, 2022) https://www.nibmindia.org/static/working_paper/NIBM_WP19_JM.pdf

under the fixed rate Reverse Repo window (forming the lower bound of the corridor). Such was the magnitude of the excess reserves that the RBI soon faced a 'collateral constraint' problem and ran out of government securities to provide to commercial banks in exchange for cash, given the fact that the window was collateralized. This forced the RBI to suspend the fixed-rate Reverse Repo window, replacing it with the non-collateralized, but interest-bearing, Statutory Deposit Facility (SDF).[66] The SDF, therefore, effectively became the new lower bound of the LAF corridor. Nevertheless, while the WACR remained the target rate under the new regime, it witnessed extreme volatility and remained below the Reverse Repo rate, and then the SDF, for a majority of the COVID years (2020 and 2021) due to excess liquidity in the system. However, as the system normalized with interest rates rising, and liquidity absorption via regular Variable Reverse Repo auctions (of multiple durations), alongside Open Market Operations (OMOs), the WACR eventually climbed to the upper extremities of the corridor – often exceeding[67] the MSF rate itself. Perhaps the most significant brunt was experienced by smaller banks, which were unable to access overnight liquidity as non-collateralized liquidity (WACR as proxy) became unsustainably expensive. Holdings of non-SLR **(see Note 3)** securities for securing collateralized loans, under the Repo facility, were also insufficient. Eventually, these banks are forced[68] to access the MSF window, which requires them to dip into their SLR portfolio,[69] often signalling inherent weaknesses to the system – reflected in their higher cost of funds[70] **(refer to Table 21)**.

66 Governor's Statement, Shashikanta Das (RBI, April 8, 2022) https://www.rbi.org.in/commonman/english/scripts/PressReleases.aspx?Id=3352

67 How Money Markets Fared in H124 (Aditya Birla Capital Mutual Fund, 2023) https://mutualfund.adityabirlacapital.com/abslamc-knowledge-centre/articles/how-have-money-markets-fared-in-h1fy24

68 Banks Step up to Borrow through MSF as Liquidity Falls (Moneycontrol, 2023) https://www.moneycontrol.com/news/business/banks-step-up-borrowing-through-msf-as-liquidity-falls-11258981.html

69 Basal III Framework on Liquidity Standards (RBI Notification, 2020) https://www.rbi.org.in/commonperson/English/Scripts/Notification.aspx?Id=3237#:~:text=As%20part%20of%20post%20Global,from%20April%201%2C%202020%5D.

70 Basal III LCR and the Operating Target of Monetary Policy: The Unintended Discord (Springer: Pattanaik et al., 2017) https://link.springer.com/article/10.1057/s41261-017-0043-2

The recent Governor's Statement[71] acknowledged the risks posed by the prevalent declines in systemic liquidity and how the RBI injected the vital reserves to keep the system in a neutral state. As specified by a highly volatile WACR, systemic liquidity shortages have always been a matter of anxiety for the Indian economy, due to a largely tight monetary stance. Recently, however, after the implementation of the GST regime **(see Note 4)**, this has developed into an even greater problem. The recent liquidity problems confronted by the Indian banking system, despite a neutral monetary policy, are a case in point. As a matter of fact, the RBI injected $41 billion in January 2025, and around $25 billion in February 2025, as part of its Variable Repo Rate (VRR) auctions[72] (of multiple short-term durations). Systemic liquidity deficit, however, remained over $18 billion since January 1st week of the current year, with the WACR often exceeding the MSF rate itself **(refer to Figure 17)**. Surprisingly, this is happening despite recent cuts in the Repo rate and credit growth being sub-optimal. This has resulted in the regular utilization of the MSF window despite large commercial banks being flush with excess reserves – reflected in the heightened demand for the SDF facility. It is to be noted that this has resulted in the regularization of the use of the LoLR facility (which is the MSF) as the facility's weekly average utilization ranges anywhere between 2 per cent and over 50 per cent of average excess reserves deposited with the RBI **(see Note 5)**. The answer to the question pertaining to why large commercial banks are unwilling to lend in the non-collateralized inter-bank market (determined by the WACR), therefore, remains elusive. A few recommendations that can be made to remedy the situation include: (1) The lowering of the lower bound (SDF) of the monetary corridor to dissuade commercial banks from depositing the majority of their excess reserves with the RBI, while ignoring the non-collateralized inter-bank fund market; (2) Supply of requisite reserves to the system to align the WACR with the prevailing Repo rate; and (3) Use of alternate securities (other than Gsecs) as collateral under the LAF for accessing funds in order to avoid collateral constraint. Decoding the first recommendation, it can be argued that commercial banks prefer the SDF primarily because

71 Governor's Statement, RBI, February 7th, 2025. https://www.rbi.org.in/Scripts/BS_PressReleaseDisplay.aspx?prid=59694

72 Weekly Statistical Supplement, RBI https://www.rbi.org.in/scripts/BS_viewWss.aspx

they are guaranteed a 'safe' fixed return on their excess reserves. Often times smaller banks, which fail to access funds via the Repo window because of collateral constraints, depend on the non-collateralized facilities, but a lack of interest from the bigger banks pushes the WACR rate near or above the upper bound of the monetary corridor. To remedy the problem, it is recommended that the lower bound (SDF facility) is lowered (remaining flexible to prevailing liquidity conditions) to disincentivize commercial banks from the overutilization of the SDF, and instead consider lending under the non-collateralized facility (given the fact that the WACR is mandated to trend near the Repo rate, which is a higher return). During the COVID years, the RBI had reduced the Reverse Repo fixed rate (before it was made dormant with the introduction of SDF) by a further 15 bps in order to dissuade commercial banks from depositing excess reserves with the RBI (as the RBI was facing collateral constraint problems at the time). When it comes to the second recommendation, RBI's weekly liquidity operations snapshot (**refer to Table 23**) reveals that the WACR is highly sensitive to the quantum of reserve supplied (utilization of the SDF window by commercial banks to park excess reserves) at certain times. While it is accepted that the end of quarter and end of financial year periods put upward pressure on the WACR, given the liquidity drawdowns as a consequence of tax payments (with Treasury General Accounts expanding), it is observed that even during the non-quarter ending periods, the WACR is often elevated. A comparison between the RBI's liquidity operations in the 1st week, and the 4th week of February 2024 (**refer to Figure 16**) reveals that in a matter of 20 days, the central bank absorptions via unconventional monetary policy tools[73] such as Variable Reverse Repo operations (of multiple durations), as well as OMOs reduced excess reserves worth $33.4 billion from the system. This exercise raised the WACR rate by 46 bps over the period, leading to a scramble at the MSF window, with small banks accessing $4.5 billion worth of liquidity (by dipping into their SLR portfolio – under the RBI's LoLR requirements).

73 Assessing the Dual Facets of Monetary Policy: profitability and Liquidity in Indian Public and Private Sector Banks (IndiaStat: Anubha Srivastava, 2024) https://www.indiastat.com/SOCIO_PDF/Assessing-Dual-Facets-Monetary-Policy-Profitability-Liquidity-Indian-Public-Private-Sector-Banks/Assessing-Dual-Facets-Monetary-Policy-Profitability.pdf

This circumstance exposes the RBI's deliberate attempt to keep the system in ex ante liquidity deficit in order to control the WACR movement – an exercise which is clearly detrimental to system health instead. It is therefore recommended that the RBI keep the system at a level where the WACR is aligned with the Repo (as originally intended) at all times by supplying sufficient liquidity whenever the former breaches a certain threshold. This can be done via targeting a range (say 6.1–6.3 per cent, when the Repo is prevailing at 6.25 per cent) beyond which WACR movements will not be tolerated, and contained immediately. The third recommendation pertains to the use of corporate bonds as an eligible collateral under the LAF. Since most commercial banks in India are involved in brokerage businesses in some form, they collectively hold almost 20 per cent of all corporate debt securities outstanding (using them for margin pledges) **(refer to Table 22)**. If the RBI allows a portion of such securities to be held as HQLA Level 1, and hence commercial bank SLR portfolio eligible, banks can utilize such holdings while borrowing under the Repo facility **(see Note 6)**. This may solve the collateral constraint problem faced by commercial banks, allowing them to be less dependent on not only the bigger banks (for the non-collateralized inter-bank fund market, driven by WACR), but also the RBI's expensive MSF window. This will also aid in keeping WACR well aligned with the Repo rate.

It can therefore be concluded that the RBI must take its 'WACR Targeting' mandate seriously (under the 2011 Monetary Framework), and must abstain from excessively narrowing the monetary corridor in the name of higher control over LM. The strategic ex ante liquidity deficit has been unsuccessful in alleviating systemic inadequacies, and reforms are the need of the hour. Perhaps a serious consideration of the aforementioned recommendations can help direct Indian monetary policy in the right direction and alignment with current market realities.[74]

74 Moneta[illegible] Policy Transmission in India under the Base Rate and MCLR Regime: A [illegible]ve Study (Nature: Chattopadhyay et al., 2023) https://www.nature.com/[illegible]99-023-01883-9

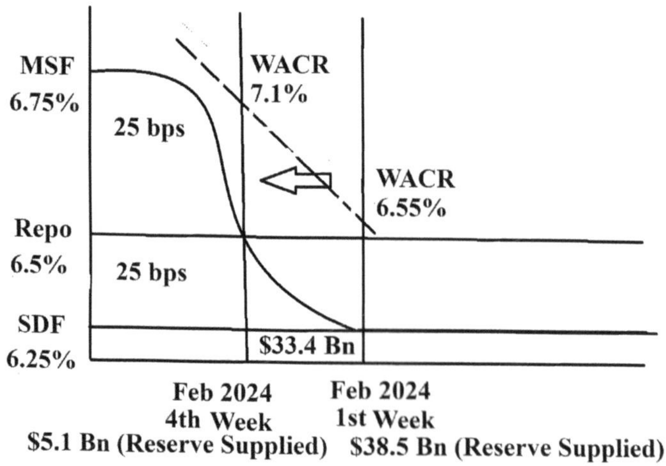

Figure 16: Snapshot of Supply of Reserve Balances in the Indian Monetary System (see Note 8).

Based on RBI data, Author's Research. Chart & Concept: Karan Mehrishi.

Table 20: Prevailing RBI Liquidity Operations Tools. Sourced from RBI data and the author's assessment

Prevailing RBI Operational Stats				
	Rate	**Collateralized**	**Function**	
Fixed Rate Repo Rate	6.25	Yes	Liquidity Infusion	Yes
Standard Deposit Facility (SDF)	6	No	Liquidity Absorption	Yes
Marginal Standing Facility (MSF)	6.5	Yes	LoLR	Yes
	Variable	Yes	LM	
14 Day + Variable Reverse Repo Rate	Variable	Yes	Long-Term LM	No
14 Day Variable Repo Rate (VRR)	Variable	Yes	LM	No

Prevailing RBI Operational Stats				
Instrument	**Rate**	**Collateralized**	**Function**	**Part of Liquidity Adjustment Facility (LAF)**
14 Day + Variable Repo Rate	Variable	Yes	Long-Term LM	No
Fixed Rate Reverse Repo Rate	Dormant	Yes	Liquidity Absorption	Dormant

Note: BIS India Institutional Framework[75]/ Chart: Author

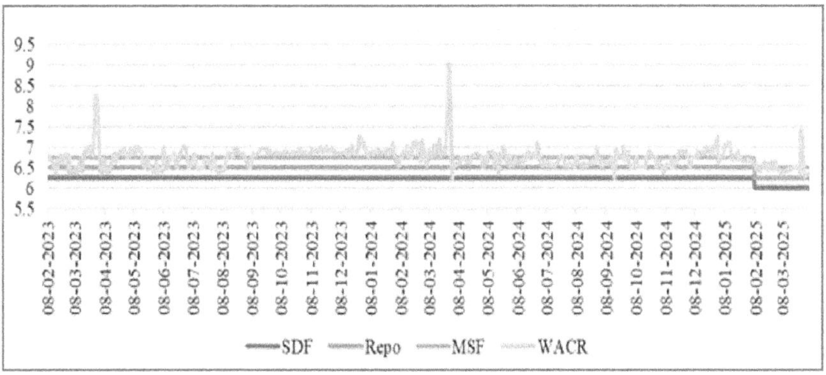

WACR Movement Within Monitory Corridor

Figure 17: WACR Movement Volatility Within the LAF. Data Source: Macrobond; Chart: Karan Mehrishi.

Table 21: Commercial Bank Cost of Funding Snapshot. Sourced from commercial bank annual reports and the author's assessment

Bank Name	Bank Size	Cost of Deposits	CASA Proportion	ROA
SBI	Large	4.81%	41%	1.36%
HDFC	Large	4.87%	38%	1.98%
ICICI	Large	4.61%	42%	2.37%
RBL	Small	6.20%	35%	0.96%
Dhanlaxmi	Small	5.30%	31%	0.38%
Karur Vyasa	Small	5.20%	30%	1.63%

75 BIS India Institutional Framework https://www.bis.org/mc/currency_areas/in.htm

Table 22: Corporate Debt Holdings Snapshot. Sourced from Commercial Bank Annual Reports, AMFI, Author's Research.

Holdings of Corporate Debt Securities (Percentage of Total Outstanding)	
RBI	~1.5%
Commercial Banks & Other Financial Institutions	~20%
Mutual Funds/ Funds of Mutual Funds	33%
Pension Funds, FPIs, among other Investors	45%

Table 23: System Liquidity/Reserve Snapshots. Sourced from RBI Weekly Statistics May 2024 (Non-Year Ending)[76] **RBI Weekly Liquidity Operations May 2024**

8. Liquidity Operations by RBI

(₹ Crore)

Date	Liquidity Adjustment Facility						Standing Liquidity Facilities	OMO (Outright)		Net Injection (+)/ Absorption (-) (1+3+5+7+9-2-4-6-8)
	Repo	Reverse Repo	Variable Rate Repo	Variable Rate Reverse Repo	MSF	SDF		Sale	Purchase	
	1	2	3	4	5	6	7	8	9	10
May. 27, 2024	-	-	75007	-	6481	68714	-	-	-	12774
May. 28, 2024	-	-	-	-	1747	79677	-	-	-	-77930
May. 29, 2024	-	-	-	-	6967	73513	-	-	-	-66546
May. 30, 2024	-	-	-	-	2776	117462	0	-	-	-114686
May. 31, 2024	-	-	50004	-	14601	84702	-	-	-	-20097
Jun. 01, 2024	-	-	-	-	9131	56402	-	-	-	-47271
Jun. 02, 2024	-	-	-	-	9095	53280	-	-	-	-44185

SDF: Standing Deposit Facility; MSF: Marginal Standing Facility.

Average Weekly MSF Demand = ₹7,257 crore
Average Weekly SDF Demand = ₹76,250 crore
WACR = 7%
MSF= 6.75%

76 RBI Weekly Data June 7th 2024 https://rbi.org.in/Scripts/WSSViewDetail.aspx?TYPE=Basic&PARAM1=6/07/2024

Table 24: February 2024 (Non-Year Ending)[77]

RBI Weekly Liquidity Operations February 2024

8. Liquidity Operations by RBI										
										(₹ Crore)
Date	Liquidity Adjustment Facility						Standing Liquidity Facilities	OMO (Outright)		Net Injection (+)/ Absorption (-) (1+3+5+7+9-2-4-6-8)
	Repo	Reverse Repo	Variable Rate Repo	Variable Rate Reverse Repo	MSF	SDF		Sale	Purchase	
	1	2	3	4	5	6	7	8	9	10
Feb. 19, 2024	-	-	-	-	2562	72929	-	-	-	-70367
Feb. 20, 2024	-	-	50003	-	1171	128324	185	-	-	-76965
Feb. 21, 2024	-	-	-	-	3965	73178	-	-	-	-69213
Feb. 22, 2024	-	-	-	-	1941	86014	146	-	-	-83927
Feb. 23, 2024	-	-	100004	-	144270	39916	-	-	-	204358
Feb. 24, 2024	-	-	-	-	57649	31924	-	-	-	25725
Feb. 25, 2024	-	-	-	-	59650	32828	-	-	-	26822
SDF: Standing Deposit Facility; MSF: Marginal Standing Facility.										

Average Weekly MSF Demand = ₹38,744 crore
Average Weekly SDF Demand = ₹66,445 crore
WACR = 7.1%
MSF = 6.75%

Table 25: March 2023 (Year Ending Liquidity)[78]

RBI Weekly Liquidity Operations March 2023

8. Liquidity Operations by RBI										
										(₹ Crore)
Date	Liquidity Adjustment Facility						Standing Liquidity Facilities	OMO (Outright)		Net Injection (+)/ Absorption (-) (1+3+5+7+9-2-4-6-8)
	Repo	Reverse Repo	Variable Rate Repo	Variable Rate Reverse Repo	MSF	SDF		Sale	Purchase	
	1	2	3	4	5	6	7	8	9	10
Mar. 27, 2023	–	–	–	–	900	103238	456	–	–	-101882
Mar. 28, 2023	–	–	–	–	623	162609	490	–	–	-161496
Mar. 29, 2023	–	–	–	–	23489	154737	1188	–	–	-130060
Mar. 30, 2023	–	–	–	–	9147	78265	–	–	–	-69118
Mar. 31, 2023	–	–	–	–	31995	233723	3900	–	–	-197828
Apr. 1, 2023	–	–	–	–	143	10721	–	–	–	-10578
Apr. 2, 2023	–	–	–	–	417	38017	–	–	–	-37600
SDF: Standing Deposit Facility; MSF: Marginal Standing Facility.										

Average Weekly MSF Demand = ₹9,531 crore
Average Weekly SDF Demand = ₹111,616 crore
WACR = 8.25%
MSF = 6.75%

77 RBI Weekly Data March 1st 2024 https://rbi.org.in/Scripts/WSSViewDetail.aspx?TYPE=Basic&PARAM1=3/01/2024

78 RBI Weekly Data April 7th 2023 https://rbi.org.in/Scripts/WSSViewDetail.aspx?TYPE=Basic&PARAM1=4/07/2023

Table 26: March 2024 (Year Ending Liquidity)[79]

RBI Weekly Liquidity Operations March 2024

8. Liquidity Operations by RBI										
										(₹ Crore)
Date	Liquidity Adjustment Facility						Standing Liquidity Facilities	OMO (Outright)		Net Injection (+)/ Absorption (-) (1+3+5+7+9-2-4-6-8)
	Repo	Reverse Repo	Variable Rate Repo	Variable Rate Reverse Repo	MSF	SDF		Sale	Purchase	
	1	2	3	4	5	6	7	8	9	10
Mar. 25, 2024	-	-	-	-	4875	76217	-	-	-	-71342
Mar. 26, 2024	-	-	100003	-	18316	114966	-	-	-	3353
Mar. 27, 2024	-	-	75002	-	31743	107677	-	-	-	-932
Mar. 28, 2024	-	-	-	-	142104	185423	-452	-	-	-43771
Mar. 29, 2024	-	-	-	-	58851	198001	-	-	-	-139150
Mar. 30, 2024	-	-	-	-	71826	254885	-	-	-	-183059
Mar. 31, 2024	-	-	-	-	65512	241763	-	-	-	-176251
SDF: Standing Deposit Facility; MSF: Marginal Standing Facility.										

Average Weekly MSF Demand = ₹56,175 crore
Average Weekly SDF Demand = ₹168,419 crore
WACR = 9%
MSF = 6.75%

Table 27: March 2025 (Year Ending Liquidity)[80]

RBI Weekly Liquidity Operations March 2025

8. Liquidity Operations by RBI										
										(₹ Crore)
Date	Liquidity Adjustment Facility						Standing Liquidity Facilities	OMO (Outright)		Net Injection (+)/ Absorption (-) (1+3+5+7+9-2-4-6-8)
	Repo	Reverse Repo	Variable Rate Repo	Variable Rate Reverse Repo	MSF	SDF		Sale	Purchase	
	1	2	3	4	5	6	7	8	9	10
Mar. 24, 2025	-	-	66215	-	279	111728	-	-	-	-45234
Mar. 25, 2025	-	-	95653	-	389	177285	0	-	-	-81243
Mar. 26, 2025	-	-	35486	-	1364	188543	-	-	44541	-107152
Mar. 27, 2025	-	-	21392	-	1114	201622	-335	-	-	-179451
Mar. 28, 2025	-	-	88424	-	7840	279056	-	-	-	-182792
Mar. 29, 2025	-	-	-	-	11653	357727	-	-	-	-346074
Mar. 30, 2025	-	-	-	-	7372	316691	-	-	-	-309319
SDF: Standing Deposit Facility; MSF: Marginal Standing Facility.										

Average Weekly MSF Demand = ₹4,287 crore
Average Weekly SDF Demand = ₹233,236 crore
WACR = 7.5%
MSF = 6.5%

79 RBI Weekly Data April 5th 2024 https://rbi.org.in/Scripts/WSSViewDetail.aspx?TYPE=Basic&PARAM1=4/05/2024

80 RBI Weekly Data April 4th 2025 https://rbi.org.in/Scripts/WSSViewDetail.aspx?TYPE=Basic&PARAM1=4/04/2025

Note 1: By narrowing the corridor, the RBI has effectively reduced the differential between the two thresholds of the monetary corridor to 50 bps, from the original 200 bps (envisioned in 2011). This has effectively made the non-collateralized inter-bank fund market (call money market) unattractive for banks as the lower threshold (SDF) of the monetary corridor is just 25 bps below the Repo rate (the middle threshold). Parking excess reserves at the SDF has therefore turned out to be lucrative for commercial banks, earning them a safe fixed return on excess reserves.

Note 2: The non-collateralized inter-bank fund market is an inter-bank fund market, determined by the WACR (or call money rate), which is similar to the Fed Fund Rate. The overnight borrowing or lending happens between two commercial banks at a certain call money rate, without the need for collateral.

Note 3: Non-SLR securities are those securities that are held in excess of the mandated securities (part of HQLA Level 1) under the SLR regulation, which requires commercial banks to hold government securities/cash equivalent to 18 per cent of NDTL. These non-SLR securities can be used by commercial banks to access the Repo window.

Note 4: The Goods and Services Tax (GST) was implemented pan-India in July 2017. The guidelines suggest that businesses must present their tax fillings and pay taxes every quarter, instead of doing it once a year (year ending on 31st March), as applicable in the previous regime. This new system, therefore, causes systemic liquidity drawdowns at the end of every quarter, as businesses pay their taxes.

Note 5: The MSF's weekly average utilization ranges anywhere between 2 per cent and over 50 per cent of average excess reserves deposited with the RBI. What this means is that average demand at the MSF window is equivalent to 2 per cent to over 50 per cent of the funds (excess reserves) being parked at the SDF window on a weekly basis.

Note 6: If the RBI allows a portion of corporate debt securities to be held as HQLA Level 1, their acceptability in the system will rise. This is because these securities will then have a status of SLR-eligible securities, which can be utilized to access funds under the Repo facility. In emergency situations, such securities can also be used under the MSF facility. Recent RBI guidelines do allow banks to hold such securities HTM, as non-SLR, but the wider acceptance in the system (as eligible collateral) is still nebulas.

Note 7: As per regulatory requirements, a commercial bank holds 18 per cent of NDTL in the form of cash or government securities. Out of this 18 per cent, 3 per cent can be used to access funds under the MSF facility, during emergency liquidity requirements.

Note 8: In Fig. 1, the RBI absorbed $33.4 billion from the system, increasing WACR by 46 bps. This shifted the supply of reserves curve to the left. What makes this scenario stand out is the fact that this happened in the month of February, which is a non-year-ending/quarter-ending month. Quarter-end months (leading to tax payments and banking liquidity falls) include March, June, September, and December.

India's Monetary Policy Stance in Accommodation & the Role of R*[81]

During the February 7th, 2025, MPC meeting, the RBI reduced the Repo rate by 25 bps,[82] and renewed its focus on economic growth, despite a persistently sticky core inflation. In the 9th April meeting, the Repo rate was further cut by 25 bps, while changing the stance to accommodative from neutral. This is a welcome move as this change in stance is connected to a slowing economy and sub-optimal credit growth (comparable to the COVID era). Nevertheless, the biggest risk faced by the economy has been systemic liquidity deficiencies (commercial banks struggling for reserves)[83] as the WACR trends higher than even the MSF Rate, the most expensive rate in

81 This is the author's original research, and part of his submitted coursework at Yale University.

82 Monetary Policy Statement, RBI, February 7th, 2025. https://www.rbi.org.in/Scripts/BS_PressReleaseDisplay.aspx?prid=59692

83 Governor's Statement, RBI, February 7th, 2025. https://www.rbi.org.in/Scripts/BS_PressReleaseDisplay.aspx?prid=59694

the system for much of first quarter of the current year **(refer to Figure 22 and Note 1).** Analysing the role of r*, or the natural rate, it is revealed that the rate is 25-bps lower than the real rate on average over a 6-year period (including the COVID phase), and that for FY2024–25, it is estimated to be still 19-bps lower, despite back-to-back rate cuts. This signals that the RBI can afford more accommodation at the system level than is currently being offered. India's persistently low output gap due to a historically tight monetary stance is another concern presented by this paper. The purpose of the section is to make a case to justify accommodative monetary policy at this time, in accordance with the needs of a fast-expanding economy that is recovering, and for better market efficiencies.

The 7th February MPC expects the Indian economy to expand by 6.4 per cent in real terms for the current financial year (ending in March 2025), based on fresh estimates from the MOSPI. This number is almost 60 bps[84] lower **(refer to Figure 25)** than the estimates presented by the Survey of Professional Forecasters (SPF) panel. The RBI is, however, convinced that a resilient 'business sentiment', rising capacity utilization levels,[85] as well as the profitability of private enterprises signal an imminent recovery, helping the economy regain its 7 per cent + growth trajectory. Concerns, however, remain regarding the external sector with possible protectionist policies imposed by the United States, India's second-largest trading partner. Exchange rate volatility due to interest rate uncertainty in the United States (due to sticky inflation and strong economic performance) is also a matter of concern for the Indian central bank, and remains a key monetary policy monitorable. Headline inflation is expected to moderate thanks to healthy reservoir levels (good monsoon providing sufficient water resources for irrigation), and the Rabi crop harvest (one of two key harvest seasons in India) hitting the market as expected. Cheap oil from Russia, as well as a possible new oil deal struck with the United States, is expected to further reduce the current account deficit, and reduce commodity-related imported inflation. Core inflation, however, remains sticky; nevertheless, the MPC decided to cut rates by 25-bps

84 Survey of Professional Forecasters (SPF), RBI, Round-92nd https://www.rbi.org.in/Scripts/PublicationsView.aspx?id=23131

85 OBICUS Survey, Q2, 2024–25, RBI, February 7th, 2025 https://www.rbi.org.in/Scripts/PublicationsView.aspx?id=23134

on 7th February, followed by another 25-bps during the 9th April policy meeting, which is justified given that the real rate is still higher than the estimated r* by 19 bps. According to RBI, Inflation is expected to fall to 4 per cent[86] for FY2025–26 (20 bps lower than the forecast of the Panel of Professional Forecasters) – exactly at the target rate (ranging 2 per cent (lower bound) −4–6 per cent (upper bound)). This positive outlook for the headline number is expected to anchor inflation expectations well, affording rate cuts. Further confidence is drawn from the fact that the Household Inflation Expectations Survey[87] shows that households expect inflation to fall both in the 3-month and 1-year horizon, suggesting that inflation expectations are well anchored. An estimation (**refer to Figure 20**) to check the policy effectiveness based on a simple Loss Function (**see Note 2 for details**) suggests that the RBI has been successful in managing the inflation-growth dynamic, with a minor uptick in inflation expected only in the January-March 2026 quarter. The Loss Function is defined as follows:

$$L(\pi, Y) = \alpha(\pi - \pi^*)\hat{}2 + \beta(y - y^*)\hat{}2, \textit{ with Parameters: } \alpha = 1.5,\ \beta = 0.3 \textit{ (RBI Estimates).}$$

Still, the Governor's Statement[88] mentioned risks posed by drawdowns in systemic liquidity, and how the RBI injected the required reserves to keep the system in the neutral state. Systemic liquidity deficiencies have always been a matter of concern for the Indian economy, due to a predominantly tight monetary stance, but recently, after the implementation of the GST regime (**see Note 3**), this has become an event bigger problem for smaller commercial banks.

Recently, the former Governor of the RBI, Shashikanta Das, was quoted as saying that r* is an 'abstract concept that cannot determine'[89]

86 Monetary Policy Statement (RBI: April 9th 2025 MPC Meeting) https://rbi.org.in/Scripts/BS_PressReleaseDisplay.aspx?prid=60176

87 Households Inflation Expectations Survey (RBI: 9th April 2025) https://www.rbi.org.in/Scripts/PublicationsView.aspx?id=23147

88 Governor's Statement, RBI, February 7th 2025. https://www.rbi.org.in/Scripts/BS_PressReleaseDisplay.aspx?prid=59694

89 Neutral Rate Cannot Determine Monetary Policy in India, Says Cen Bank Chief (Reuters, July 19, 2024) https://www.reuters.com/world/india/neutral-

India's monetary policy. Nevertheless, there has been a consensus among India's MPC Members that India's real rate should preferably be around 1 per cent[90] for an ideal growth-inflation trade-off. Therefore, while there is no mention of r*, over the years, especially after COVID-19, India's MPC has been treating the 1 per cent real rate as its target rate. It is, however, felt that no matter how irrelevant India's central bank considers the r*, the concept cannot be ignored in a domestic demand-driven economy that experiences high inflation, low liquidity (supply of capital), and low efficiency, despite expanding at 7 per cent on average in real terms. In its July 2024 Monthly Bulletin, the RBI (Behera, 2024)[91] did present its views on the estimated r* for India, and utilized various techniques, including Laubach-Williams (LW) and DSGE models. Consequently, the RBI economists suggest that the current r* for India is in the range of 1.4–1.9 per cent. Based on these numbers, it was claimed that post-COVID, the potential output growth has been high, which has pushed the natural rate upwards. It is also advised that high demand for capital, lower savings, and high government expenditure have pushed the natural rate upwards, which is described by the RBI as being a good thing for the economy. This claim nonetheless signals a stressed economy, with little breathing space. Nevertheless, given this context, using similar parameters (as presented by the RBI) for both inflation and output gap, an attempt has been made to estimate the r* for India to provide an alternative hypothesis. Accordingly, the standard Taylor rule equation is then utilized with one additional component, pertaining to the exchange rate, using the gamma parameter utilized by the RBI for stock market performance. While the standard components pertaining to inflation and output would have been sufficient,

---

rate-cannot-determine-monetary-policy-india-says-cenbank-chief-2024-07-19/#:~:text=The%20central%20bank%20in%20its,referring%20to%20the%20latest%20study.

90 Real Rate of About 1% Appropriate For Indian Economy: Rate Panel's Goyal (Reuters, February 23rd 2023) https://www.reuters.com/world/india/real-interest-rate-about-1-appropriate-indian-economy-rate-panels-goyal-2023-02-23/

91 RBI Monthly Bulletin, July 2024: Updating Estimates of the Natural Rate of Interest for India with Post-Pandemic Evidence (Behera, 2024) https://rbidocs.rbi.org.in/rdocs/Bulletin/PDFs/0BULLETINJULY18072024C1D39FE2E7AB4F8893C8E207C7818398.PDF

it was felt that exchange rates (especially pertaining to the USD) would be relevant for an economy that faces a current account deficit and is primarily a newly industrialized economy. The standard Taylor rule was then rearranged for the purpose, after estimating the output gap (log weighted) **(see Note 8)**, inflation gap, as well as the exchange rate gap for India. The Taylor Rule Standard Equation is presented as follows:

$$\mathbf{i} = \pi + r^* + 1.5\,(\pi - \pi^*) + 0.3\,(y - y^*) + 0.8(Ex - Ex^*).$$

Rearranging for r*:

$$r^* = i - \pi - 1.5(\pi - \pi^*) - 0.3(y - y^*) - 0.8(Ex - Ex^*)$$

Refer to **Note 7** for Model Parameters.

The results show that India's r* has been in the vicinity of **1.67** per cent (2024–25 Estimates), with the real rate average being 1.96 per cent, in the same period, equating to a 29-bps differential. In fact, over a 6-year period under consideration, the r* has actually been 25-bps below the real rate, indicating that India's monetary policy is restrictive, and focusing on inflation control, at the cost of output growth. While the RBI does not provide the average r* for the year for India, it can be argued that the official number will be around this number, given the prior estimates ranging 1.4–1.9 per cent. Nevertheless, in its assessment of r*, the RBI considers 3-month T-Bill yield, Bombay Stock Exchange (BSE) Sensex, as well as bank credit/ credit growth, as additional variables, and hence the numbers are slightly different. India's r* estimate, however, seems to be low, given the fact that BIS estimates that China's r* is in the range of 2–3 per cent.[92] Since China has an economy that is over four times that of India, and has significantly more supply of capital, there seems to be an undefined variable that is putting downward pressure on India's natural rate. An argument can be made regarding the higher productivity in China, leading to a higher r*, but Indian productivity lies in services, unlike China's focus on manufacturing. Therefore, productivity comparison in both countries does not count in this context

92 Natural Interest Rate in China (BIS Working Paper, June 2021) https://www.bis.org/publ/work949.htm#:~:text=Findings,mirrors%20that%20in%20other%20economies.

(Federal Reserve Bank of St. Louis explanation on the subject).[93] Making sense of this, the Federal Reserve Bank of New York paper 'Safety, Liquidity, and Natural Rate of Interest'[94] by Del Negro et al. sheds some light on the subject. The authors cite the 2012 works of Krishnamurthy and Jorgensen,[95] where the economists propose the concept of 'Convenience Yields', which explains the investor preference for Government securities (Gsecs) for their relative 'safety, and liquidity'. This is perhaps based on the works of former Federal Reserve Governor Ben Bernanke,[96] who explained the rise in global demand for US Government securities in his 'savings glut hypothesis'. Del Negro et al. explain this by the Euler Equation[97]:

$$(\mathbf{R_t}): 1 = E_t\left[\frac{1+R_t}{1+\pi_{t+1}}(1+CY_{t+1})M_{t+1}\right]^{98}$$

Where, $1+CY_{t+1}$ represents the convenience yield (as presented by Del Negro et al./ Krishnamurthy et al.), and M_{t+1} is the discount factor. Increasing convenience yields are claimed to 'reduce the natural rate by 1 per cent'. Given the fact that the Indian collateral market in the banking system is almost 100 per cent driven by Government securities, the concept of convenience yields arguably does explain India's lower than usual natural rate. In fact, a

93 The Manufacturing Sector's Evolution and its Role in an Economy (Federal Reserve Bank of St. Louis) https://www.stlouisfed.org/on-the-economy/2018/march/manufacturing-sectors-evolution-role-economy#:~:text=The%20authors%20noted%20that%20this,rapid%20as%20the%20manufacturing%20sector's.%E2%80%9D

94 Federal Reserve Bank of New York Working Paper: 'Safety, Liquidity, and Natural Rate of Interest' (Del Negro et al.) https://www.newyorkfed.org/research/staff_reports/sr812.html

95 The Aggregate Demand for Treasury Debt: University of Chicago (Krishnamurthy, and Jorgensen, 2012) https://www.journals.uchicago.edu/doi/abs/10.1086/666526

96 Governor Speech on the Global Savings Glut and the US Current Account Deficit (Yale School of Management, 2005) https://elischolar.library.yale.edu/cgi/viewcontent.cgi?article=5269&context=ypfs-documents

97 Federal Reserve Bank of New York Working Paper: 'Safety, Liquidity, and Natural Rate of Interest' (Del Negro et al.) https://www.newyorkfed.org/research/staff_reports/sr812.html

98 The Aggregate Demand for Treasury Debt: University of Chicago (Krishnamurthy, and Jorgensen, 2012) https://www.journals.uchicago.edu/doi/abs/10.1086/666526

significant correlation between 3-month T-Bill yields, and r* suggests that whenever short-term yields fall (when Repo is not changed), the condition equates to lower issuance of Government short-term debt **(see Note 4)**. This in turn may be a signal of a 'collateral constraint/insufficient collateral' (marking even higher preference for Government securities) that reduces r* incessantly in India **(see Note 5)**. This artificially low r* for India perhaps raises questions pertaining to the economy's inherent problems masked by a highly liquid Government securities market. Nevertheless, the r* is now showing signs of increases, rising 10 bps **(refer to Figure 18)** for 2025–26 estimates. The recent liquidity problems faced by the Indian banking system, despite an accommodative monetary policy, are a case in point. As a matter of fact, the RBI injected $41 billion in January 2025, and around $25 billion in February 2025, as part of its VRR auctions[99] (of multiple short-term durations). Systemic liquidity deficit has therefore remained over $18 billion since January 1st week of the current year. Surprisingly, this is happening despite recent cuts in the Repo rate and credit growth being sub-optimal. One argument has been that end-of-quarter tax payments have caused systemic liquidity to decline, but the GST (demanding quarterly tax payments) was implemented in India only after 2017. An analysis **(refer to Figure 23)** of WACR, as a proxy for demand for reserves in the system, and the estimated r*, however, suggests that there has been a historic positive correlation (by way of direction of movement on average) between the two variables (even though their differential is significant). What this means is that when WACR is high, households may also be demanding (in addition to RBI's liquidity absorption) a higher rate of return to supply their savings for the purpose of investment (natural state). Post-COVID-19, this relationship became even stronger because of pent-up demand (driving up consumption) and high inflationary pressures due to supply-chain shocks. Based on the earlier analysis involving the Taylor Rule (along with a combined effect of Convenience Yields), it can be argued that the RBI can afford to be more accommodative than restrictive, since the r* remains 25 bps lower on average (despite recent uptick), as compared to the real rate. This will not only allow the system to access cheaper liquidity from the RBI but also remain less stressed during normal market conditions (which in India is often not

99 Weekly Statistical Supplement, RBI https://www.rbi.org.in/scripts/BS_viewWss.aspx

the case). Liquidity targeting, therefore, becomes important here (by keeping the WACR rate near the Repo Rate). Secondly, since it can be argued that Convenience Yields may play an important role in putting downward pressure on India's r*, there is a possibility that an expanding economy may utilize the use of alternative securities for collaterals (like in developed economies) in the future. Such securities (including corporate debt securities) may take away some of the advantages accorded by the use of government securities, exclusively. Continued fiscal expansion may also increase Government debt issuance, reducing the effect of Convenience Yields. This in turn can raise India's r* in the near term, and a sudden increase (due to a policy change) may take the system by surprise. The RBI must therefore keep the system in accommodation mode so that sudden rate increases on the back of a higher natural rate may not lead to a liquidity shock. Inflation targeting has, anyway, helped anchor inflation expectations, and any inflationary fallout because of this stance can be easily contained by active reserve management. This brings us to the point pertaining to neglect of the output gap in India's monetary policy. India's actual GDP growth is suboptimal, and this is clearly showcased by the output gap[100] now falling to 0.8 per cent (in 2024–25), declining from 1.4 per cent, recorded over the previous three years (see **Figure 19**). In the United States, the output gap has now risen to 1.8 per cent[101] (in 2024), the highest since the COVID era on the back of strong productivity growth. This perhaps makes an additional case to not have a prolonged restrictive monetary policy, while maintaining an ex-ante liquidity deficit stance. Instead, the situation calls for a more accommodative stance, and at least one more rate cut.

It can therefore be concluded from the above analysis that the r* indeed plays an important role in India's monetary policy, and management of systemic liquidity situation – policymakers therefore must pay heed. The current situation faced by a slowing economy (post-COVID), despite the RBI's valiant efforts, calls for innovative solutions. While most of such solutions are fiscal, and not a prerogative of the RBI, the central bank's current

100 India's Output Gap Now Positive: RBI Bulletin (Moneycontrol.com, 2023) https://www.moneycontrol.com/news/business/economy/rbi-bulletin-indias-output-gap-now-positive-stagflation-risk-at-only-3-11211891.html

101 Fred Data on US Output Gap https://fred.stlouisfed.org/graph/?g=f1cZ

monetary stance, becoming accommodative (which it should maintain for the time being), is a well-thought-out strategy to build market confidence and allow itself to make better policy choices in advance.

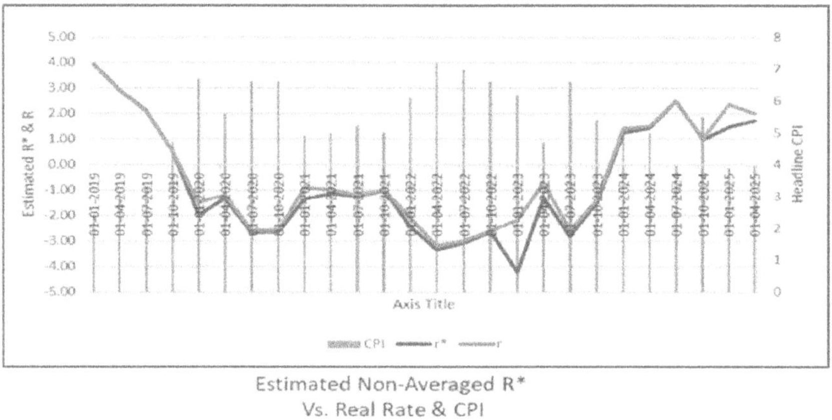

Figure 18: Depicting the estimated non-averaged R* evolution as compared to the Real Repo Rate and CPI.

Sourced from Author Estimates for r. Data Source: Macrobond. Chart: Karan Mehrishi.*

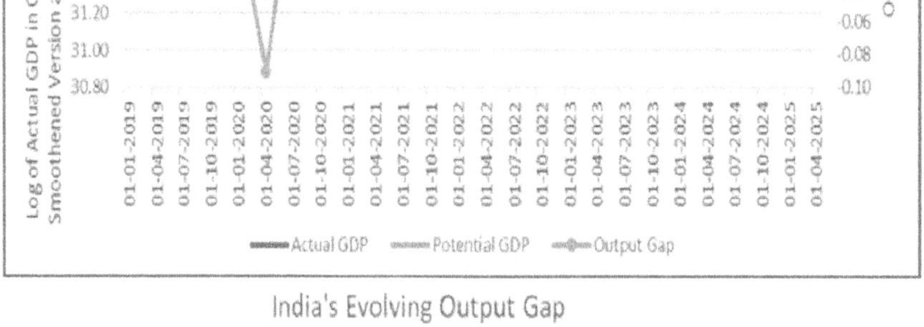

Figure 19: Depicting India's evolving output gap during and after the pandemic.

Sourced from Author's Research; Data Source: Macrobond. Chart: Karan Mehrishi.

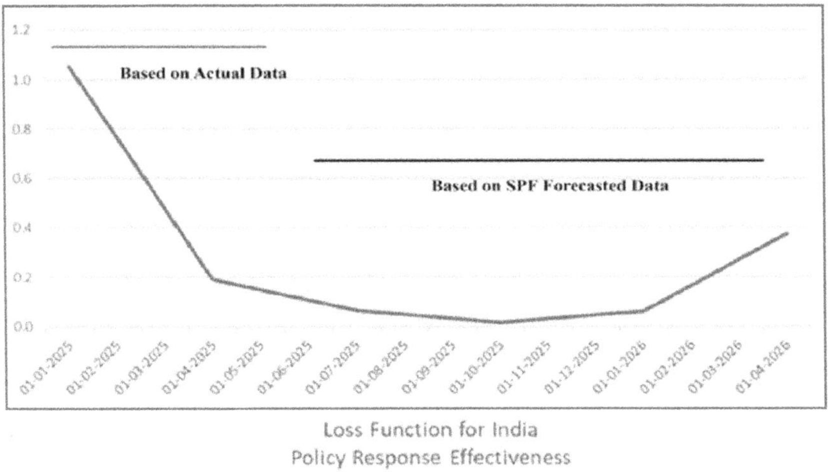

Figure 20: Loss Function estimates for the assessment of policy response effectiveness.

Refer to Note 2. Sourced from Author's Research & Estimates. Chart: Karan Mehrishi.

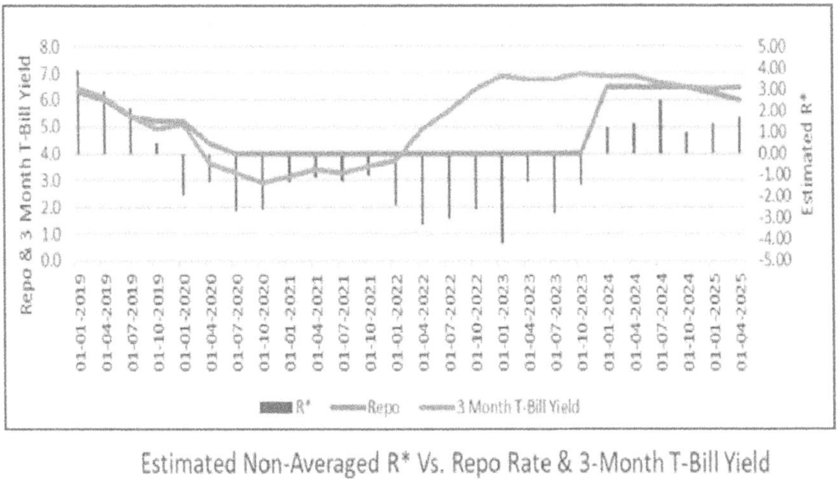

Figure 21: Depicting the evolution of the estimated non-averaged R* as compared to the prevailing Repo Rate, and 3-month T-Bill yield.

Data Sourced from Macrobond; Author's Research. Chart: Karan Mehrishi.

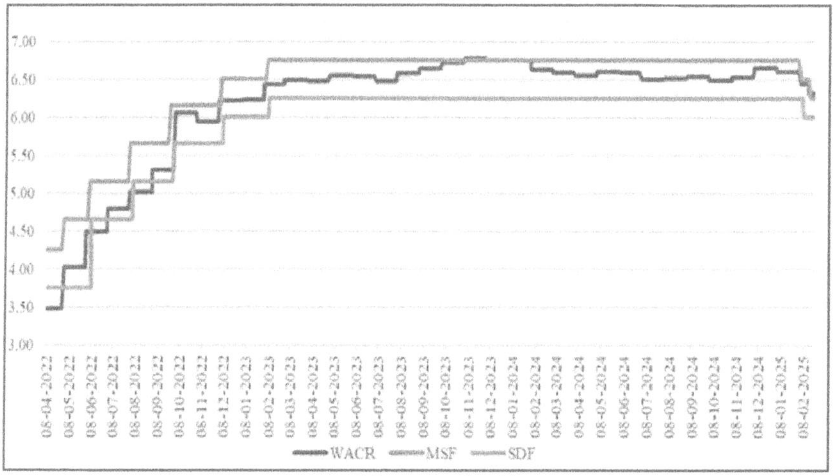

Monetary Corridor

Call Money Rate WACR Vs. Statutory Deposit Facility Rate

Figure 22: Depicting the Indian monetary corridor dynamic post the pandemic.

Refer to Note 1. Data Sourced from Macrobond. Chart: Karan Mehrishi. Note: SDF: Statutory Deposit Facility Rate; MSF: Marginal Standing Facility Rate.

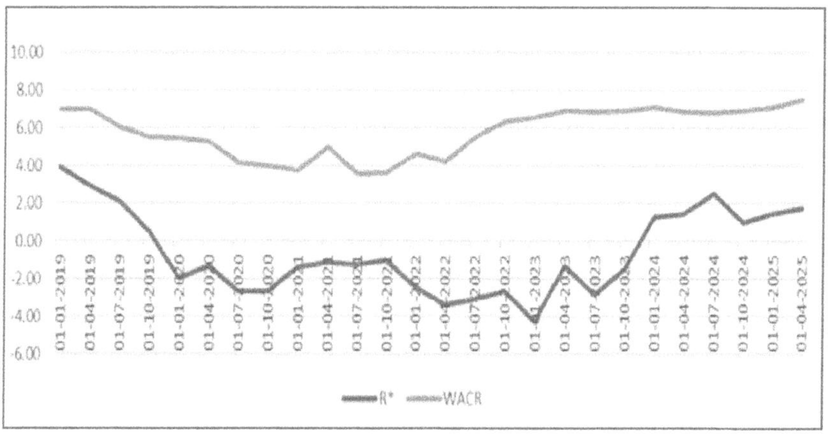

Estimated Non-Averaged R* Vs. WACR

Figure 23: Depicting estimated non-averaged R* evolution as compared to the prevailing WACR.

Sourced from Macrobond; Chart: Karan Mehrishi.

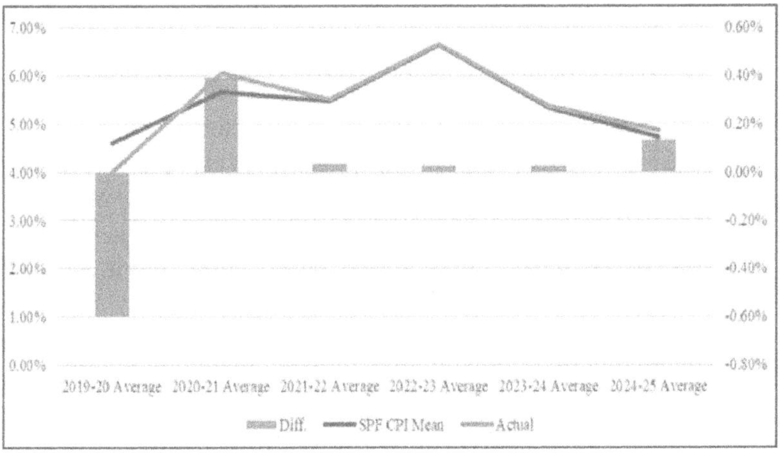

SPF Expectatation Vs. Actual CPI

Figure 24: Depicting SPF (Survey of Professional Forecasters) Estimates Vs. Actual Headline CPI during and after the pandemic. Assessing forecaster accuracy and data predictability.

Sourced from RBI Data. Chart: Karan Mehrishi.

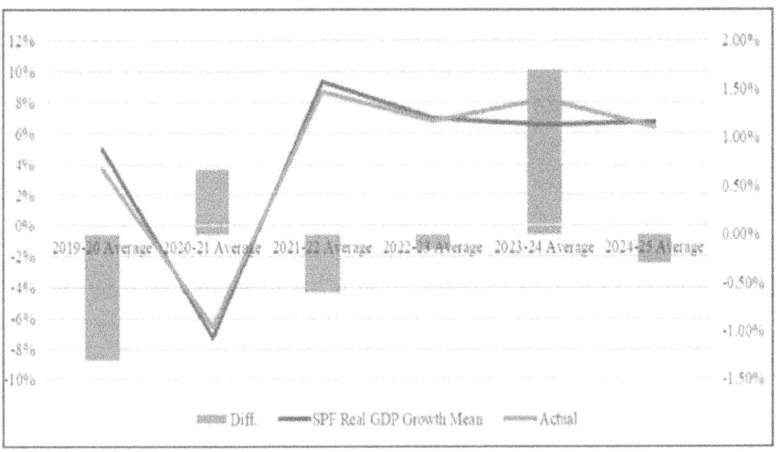

SPF Expectation Vs. Actual GDP Growth

Figure 25: Depicting SPF (Survey of Professional Forecasters) Estimates Vs. Actual GDP Growth during and after the pandemic. Assessing forecaster accuracy and data predictability.

Sourced from RBI Data. Chart: Karan Mehrishi.

Note 1: Historic low efficiencies, capacity constraints, and demand-supply mismatches have caused persistent inflationary pressures in the Indian economy. As a consequence, a tight monetary policy stance has been the mainstay of the RBI. In this context, the central bank has maintained one of the smallest balance sheets (about 22 per cent of GDP) among G20 (and therefore a low M0 to GDP ratio), and kept interest rates high. The system is also kept in deficit by absorbing excess liquidity via OMOs, and Reverse & Variable Reverse Repo Operations. With a persistently high Reverse Repo Rate (which is just 25 bps lower than the Repo Rate), and now the SDF, the RBI has given large commercial banks a lucrative avenue to park their reserves with the central bank, instead of lending it out to either smaller banks (under non-collateralized call money market), or borrowers with riskier profiles. Since India's capital markets are underdeveloped (providing liquidity to only GSecs or AAA/AA rated corporate debt in the secondary market), smaller commercial banks with lower ratings are often unable to raise money elsewhere. This has resulted in downward pressure on the supply of liquidity in the system, with smaller banks often struggling for liquidity and often knocking on the RBI's MSF window, which is 25 bps more expensive than the Repo window. This, in turn, has raised the cost of capital in India, with commercial banks often charging mark-ups to maintain their NIMs. Households and lower-rated corporate borrowers (which are the majority) are the most impacted. The condition is somewhat agnostic to monetary policy and is structural in nature.

Note 2: The simple loss function: $\mathbf{L}\ (\pi, \mathbf{Y}) = \alpha\ (\pi - \pi^*)\text{\textasciicircum}2 + \beta\ (\mathbf{y} - \mathbf{y}^*)\text{\textasciicircum}2$, with Parameters: $\alpha = 1.5$, $\beta = 0.3$ (from RBI estimates, presented by Behera 2024) was built to assess the policy effectiveness of the RBI, given a certain level of inflation and growth. The model uses the difference between the actual inflation rate and the target inflation rate for inflation, and the difference between actual GDP growth and smoothened GDP growth for the GDP growth rate. The lower the loss function output (near to 0), the better. The Loss Function is based on 6 quarter data (with two quarters of actual data (last 2 quarters of the previous Financial Year 2024–25), and four quarters of SPF[102] estimated data (all 4 quarters of the current Financial Year 2025–26)). Fig. 3 shows how well the RBI managed the growth-inflation trade-off, and the Loss Function has remained near 0. The design of the Loss Function is a simplified version of the models presented in the IMF Working Paper: Designing a Simple Loss Function for Central Banks (Debortoli et al.).[103]

Note 3: The GST was implemented pan-India in July 2017. The guidelines suggest that businesses must present their tax filings, and pay taxes every quarter, instead of doing it once a year (year ending on 31st March), as applicable in the previous regime. This new system, therefore, causes systemic liquidity drawdowns at the end of every quarter, as businesses pay their taxes.

Note 4: This is my own intuition based on data analysis pertaining to 3 Month T-Bill Yields, WACR, and Repo rates.

Note 5: The idea for the application of convenience yields to India was spawned by the Federal Reserve Bank of New York Paper, 'Liquidity Policy and Systemic Risk'[104] by Adrian et al., who argue that 'low levels of risk-free assets make liquidity requirements expensive'. The analysis is on liquidity requirements and the cost of capital for financial intermediaries. Since we are talking about systemic liquidity in India, a relation between low r* in India and convenience yields made sense. Nevertheless, more research is required to fully understand such a relationship, scientifically. A brief discussion by Liberty Street Economics, 'A Look at Convenience Yields Across the World',[105] also presents an interesting point of view in this regard.

102 Forward Looking Survey: SPF Forecasts Round 93 (RBI) https://www.rbi.org.in/Scripts/PublicationsView.aspx?id=23144

103 IMF Working Paper: Designing a Simple Loss Function for Central Banks (Debortoli et al.) (Downloadable Version on the IMF site)

104 Federal Reserve Bank of New York Paper, 'Liquidity Policy and Systemic Risk' (Adrian et al.) https://www.newyorkfed.org/medialibrary/media/research/staff_reports/sr661.pdf

105 Liberty Street Economics, 'A Look at Convenience Yields Across the World' (Diamond, and Tassel) https://libertystreeteconomics.newyorkfed.org/2023/10/a-look-at-convenience-yields-around-the-world/

Note 6: Short-term systemic liquidity in India is measured by the WACR rate, or weekly net absorptions/infusions (data provided by RBI Weekly Supplement). Nevertheless, the r^* is a broader metric, given that it represents the structural situation of the economy, pertaining to its productivity, economic performance, and a predominantly GSec (risk-free) driven collateral market. This is the intuition in the context of the argument.

Note 7: Ex = Exchange Rate. Parameters: Our Estimates use parameters used by the RBI Estimates, i.e., $\alpha = 1.5$, $\beta = 0.3$. Meanwhile, $\gamma = 0.8$ parameter is used from RBI estimates as well, though this parameter was used by the RBI for a different variable (i.e., stock market performance).

Note 8: For Output Gap, the GDP at Constant Prices (Actual Output) was sourced from Macrobond Data. The series was then smoothened using the Exponential Smoothing tool (as an alternate to the HP Filter) to get a smoothened series (Potential Output). Both series were then put in Log form. The difference was the Output Gap.

Structural Reforms in the Indian Monetary System & Future Readiness[106]

The purpose of this section is to present a case for structural reforms in the Indian monetary system, especially pertaining to the acceptance of alternative collaterals. Under the current regime, government securities are perhaps the only acceptable/good collateral. As a remedy, this author recommends that the RBI start accepting BBB and overrated corporate debt as acceptable/good collateral, and assume the role of a Market Maker of Last Resort (MMLR) to signal confidence to market actors. Additionally, RBI must plan for the future and start developing alternative collateral classes in expectation of

106 This is the author's original research, and part of his submitted coursework at Yale University.

future collateral constraint problems faced by commercial banks, in light of rising foreign demand for Indian government securities (especially since the COVID-19 era). When India gained independence, the ruling government of the time found it safe to depend on domestic savings for deficit financing, and banks were mobilized for the purpose. As a regulating entity, the RBI was in turn tasked to be a ringmaster of the system. Since then, Indian commercial banks have accordingly built their balance sheets on government securities, which largely inhabit their asset side. This leaves insufficient room for forex holdings and corporate debt securities, provisioned as collateral. Moreover, utilizing innovative tools such as Statutory Liquidity Ratio (SLR), the Indian Government and the RBI have been in cahoots to force feed banks with a continuous supply of government securities. Consequently, over the years, the Government has created a bunch of 'too big to fail' commercial banks to run a closed-ended monetary system, which is tasked to finance government debt, and allow fiscal deficits to be maintained sustainably. These banks have, in turn, cornered a majority of public deposits, allowing them to become formidable financiers of the government. Resultantly, these banks have significant influence on both the overnight money market and LM, leaving smaller market players at their mercy. With large public deposit bases inhabiting their liability sides, these banks are free to build a large asset side inhabited by government securities (apart from loan assets). On its part, the RBI, which is the administrator of these commercial banks, ensures system-wide receptivity by recognizing government securities as the ultimate weapon, as collateral. RBI's own balance sheet has virtually no trace of private debt, and therefore, NDA,[107] are almost completely built up of government securities. What this means is that such securities are the only instruments of exchange under the RBI's collateralized window, and there is virtually no liquidity for any other instrument type in India's entire monetary system. This arrangement has created significant problems for the Indian financial system by restricting the development of a credible secondary market for corporate debt securities and municipal bonds. Indian mutual funds have emerged as the primary holders of non-government debt, but redemption pressures often force them to either sell their asset holdings

107 RBI Annual Reports (2023–24)

at significant haircuts or, worse, wind down their funds in their entirety. Eligible corporate issuers also find it difficult to raise money in the capital market, and are majorly dependent on bank loans as the primary source of funding for their capital expenditure or working capital requirements. The situation has not only resulted in significantly high cost of capital in India but also a lack of diversified funding sources for corporations, municipalities, and non-government (quasi) entities.

According to the RBI's Master Circular on Basel 3 – Capital Regulations,[108] Indian commercial banks are permitted to maintain corporate debt securities (issued by non-financial entities) within the High-Quality Liquid Assets (HQLA) framework. While Level 1 of such assets is primarily reserved for government debt securities and free cash, Level 2 provisions are more corporate debt-friendly. The regulations suggest that commercial banks can inhabit 40 per cent of the HQLA Level 2 category with corporate debt that is rated a minimum AA (for Level 2A), and BBB (for Level 2B), albeit with a haircut (ranging between 15 and 50 per cent of 'current market value of the held asset'). Despite the provisions, risk of higher haircuts, and low liquidity forces commercial banks are forced to inhabit almost the entire HQLA portfolio with government securities, which attract a 0 per cent risk weight, and are widely tradable. Consequently, today, commercial banks in India are the biggest hoarders of government securities (39 per cent of total outstanding,[109] compared to US banks that hold just 6 per cent of such securities, outstanding, as represented in **Table 28/29**). Another important reason for this low interest pertains to the 'non-collateral-status' for non-government securities in the Indian monetary system (under the FALLCR regime^^). This makes India a closed-ended monetary system based on government securities, exclusively, as collateral. While commercial banks do hold over $100 billion worth of corporate debt securities (as part of their brokerage businesses), the RBI itself, as a system administrator, barely holds any corporate debt on its own balance sheet. Therefore, such securities

108 Basel III Framework on Liquidity Standards – Liquidity Coverage Ratio (LCR), Liquidity Risk Monitoring Tools and LCR Disclosure Standards: https://www.rbi.org.in/commonman/english/Scripts/Notification.aspx?Id=2490

109 NCAER: India's Debt Dilemma (Eichengreen, Gupta 2023): https://www.ncaer.org/wp-content/uploads/2023/07/Paper-I-Barry-Poonam.pdf

have little acceptance under the RBI's LAF window. Unless this happens, the acceptability of corporate debt as collateral will not become mainstream in India. Parallels can be run here with the holding of 23 per cent.[110] of all Mortgage-Backed Securities (MBS) outstanding by the US Federal Reserve, in conjunction with commercial banks that hold an estimated 32 per cent[111] of such securities on their balance sheets. This holding of mutually acceptable securities adds depth to the collateral market and allows for seamless liquidity transfusion within the system. The RBI must therefore start with accepting BBB- and above-rated corporate debt securities, as 'good collateral' to add volume to the segment. According to CRISIL data,[112] BBB (investment grade and above) category represents 52 per cent of the entire corporate debt universe in India, and this amounts to ~$290 billion. While this number is minuscule as compared to the $1.2 trillion worth[113] of government securities held by banks as part of their HQLA/excess HQLA, corporate debt's mainstream acceptance at the collateralized windows will be a step in the right direction. One way of increasing confidence in the market is by the RBI assuming the role of the Market Maker of Last Resort (MMLR),[114] as a backstop arrangement. Given the quantum of eligible debt being very small (to cause any systemic risk problems during crises) at this time, the RBI must begin to strengthen the system for the future. For this to happen effectively, the RBI must carry a quantum of 10 per cent ** of investment-grade corporate debt securities (equivalent to ~$29 billion at this time), as inventory on its balance sheet, at all times, under the provisions of a permanent stabilization fund. The RBI can then use these holdings not

110 Federal Reserve Bank of New York: Staff Report: Mortgage-Backed Securities (MBS) (Fuster et al.): https://www.newyorkfed.org/medialibrary/media/research/staff_reports/sr1001.pdf

111 Federal Reserve Bank of New York: Staff Report: Mortgage-Backed Securities (MBS) (Fuster et al.): https://www.newyorkfed.org/medialibrary/media/research/staff_reports/sr1001.pdf

112 CRISIL Ratings: Default Ratings Transitions Study (Fiscal 2022): https://www.crisilratings.com/content/dam/crisil/our-analysis/publications/default-study/crisil-ratings-annual-default-and-ratings-transition-study-fy-2022.pdf

113 Author's calculations based on budgetary documents (net debt outstanding)

114 BIS: Can emerging economy central banks be market makers of last resort? (Michael Dooley): https://www.bis.org/publ/bppdf/bispap79k.pdf

only for price stabilization, but also to replace stressed/defaulted securities during times of crises. Additionally, inclusion of municipal bonds in the said fund should also be considered, given the poor financial health of India's 232 municipal corporations, which have a total issuance outstanding of just $500 million[115] (compared to America's $4.1 trillion[116]), at this time. The municipal bonds market must be developed by increasing its acceptance in the system, and unless the RBI does not confer 'collateral status' to these instruments, things will not change for the better. Currently, highest rated Indian municipal bonds are penalized by a risk premium of over 300 bps[117] on average, as compared to similar-duration government securities (compared to just 34 bps[118] in the US for 10-year Gsec/AAA municipal bonds). This will give the market adequate confidence that the RBI is ready to backstop any eventuality in the future. As the corporate debt market develops further, and the system becomes more sophisticated, a diversified collateral market will be the key in lowering the cost of capital in India[119] (as presented in **Figure 28**), as, which is yet another aspect in this discussion. In recent times, due to low acceptance (as collateral, and limited tradability in the secondary market)[120] of corporate debt securities within the system, corporates raising money in the capital market had to deal with significant risk premiums demanded by investors. Compared to a similar duration government debt security, Indian BBB-rated corporate debt securities are penalized with a

115 RBI: Report on Municipal Finances 2024: https://m.rbi.org.in/scripts/AnnualPublications.aspx?head=Report%20on%20Municipal%20Finances

116 SIFMA: US Municipal Bond Statistics: https://www.sifma.org/resources/research/statistics/us-municipal-bonds-statistics/

117 RBI: Report on Municipal Finances 2024: https://m.rbi.org.in/scripts/AnnualPublications.aspx?head=Report%20on%20Municipal%20Finances

118 Nuveen (TIAA): Municipal Market: Bonds are acting as bonds again: https://www.nuveen.com/en-us/insights/municipal-bond-investing/municipal-market-bonds-are-acting-like-bonds-again

119 Inspiration: NBER Working Paper: INVESTMENT AND THE COST OF CAPITAL: NEW EVIDENCE FROM THE CORPORATE BOND MARKET (Gilchrist, Zakrajsek, 2007): https://www.nber.org/system/files/working_papers/w13174/w13174.pdf

120 IMF: Corporate Debt Market: Evolution, Prospects, and Policy (Surti, Goel, 2023): https://www.elibrary.imf.org/display/book/9798400223525/CH005.xml

risk premium of over 600 bps[121] on average. In comparison, the US BBB risk premium (over equivalent government security) has been just under 160 bps on average (**Figures 26 and 27**). Indian mutual funds are perhaps the primary holders of corporate debt securities, and have been playing an important role in stabilizing the market, given the limited takers elsewhere. Consequently, the fixed income MFs hold 33 per cent or $185 billion[122] worth of corporate debt securities, out of the total outstanding of roughly $559 billion.[123] In comparison, the US fixed income MFs hold just 13 per cent or $1.4 trillion worth of corporate debt securities, out of a total outstanding of $11 trillion.[124] Therefore, in conjunction with its MMLR function, as well as establishing investment grade corporate debt securities as a 'good collateral', the RBI must formulate a 'tripartite-collateralized-liquidity-facility', that involves MFs, along with commercial banks. This will allow the system's biggest holders of corporate debt to trade their securities with both commercial banks and the RBI. This arrangement will not only add liquidity to the corporate debt market but also add depth to the secondary market. Of course, this would mean higher regulatory oversight (collateral quality standards) on MFs, but overall system stability will be much more robust, especially during a crisis. Finally, as Indian sovereign debt becomes part of global indexes such as JP Morgan Chase,[125] chances are that banks will have to reduce their government securities holdings, as a proportion of total outstanding. This adjustment will happen as foreign portfolio investors increase their holdings, given the index-related capital inflows (and ability to offer better deals to existing holders via lower haircuts in the secondary market). Already, over the past one-year, foreign portfolio investor ownership of Indian government securities (because of index inclusions) has doubled to

121 Author's calculations based on SEBI & NSDL data

122 Author's calculations based on Association of Mutual Funds in India (AMFI) data: https://www.amfiindia.com/indian-mutual

123 NSDL: India Bond Info: https://www.indiabondinfo.nsdl.com/

124 SIFMA: US Corporate Bond Statistics: https://www.sifma.org/resources/research/statistics/us-corporate-bonds-statistics/

125 India's growing capital market: Promising first steps to internationalization (S&P Global) https://www.spglobal.com/en/research-insights/special-reports/india-forward/indias-growing-capital-market-promising-first-steps-to-internationalization

2.3 per cent,[126] and this number is expected to go up, as more global indexes include Indian debt. To compensate, it is necessary that the RBI gets prepared for possible collateral constraints emerging in the near future. Early preparation would mean wider acceptance of alternative asset classes, the size of which is set to rise with higher issuances, given the appetite of the Indian economy, currently growing by 10 per cent (in nominal terms), on average, annually.

It is, therefore, clear that the Indian monetary system and its collateral management, have not undergone any structural reforms since the passing of the 1949 Banking Regulations Act. This came to light during the inadequacies faced by the system during the COVID period. Rapid changes in the Indian financial market and demand for alternative funding sources consequently create a need for reformations and the redefining of the 'good collateral' by the RBI for the sake of the fast-evolving economy.

***Assumption based on the RBI holding 10 per cent of government securities, outstanding. ^^FALLCR (Facility to Avail Liquidity for LCR): SLR carveout[127] equivalent to 16 per cent of NDTL that can be utilized for the computation of LCR during crises. Eligible assets are GSecs (As per HQLA Level 1 standards).*

Table 28: Who Holds Indian Government Securities?

Government Securities Holders	US	India
Central Bank	20%	10%
Banking Institutions	6%	39%
Mutual Funds Debt Focus	16%	1.5%
Others (Pension Funds, FPIs, etc.)	58%	50%

Sourced from SIFMA, RBI, BIS; Author's Calculations.

126 India's growing capital market: Promising first steps to internationalization (S&P Global) https://www.spglobal.com/en/research-insights/special-reports/india-forward/indias-growing-capital-market-promising-first-steps-to-internationalization

127 BIS: Basal 3 Liquidity Framework - Implementation and Way Forward (Vishwanathan, 2015) https://www.bis.org/review/r160111a.pdf

Table 29: Who Holds Indian Corporate Debt?

India Corporate Debt Holdings (% of Total)	
Central Bank	1–2%
Banking Institutions (non-SLR/Excess HQLA#)	~20%*
Mutual Funds	33%
Others (FPIs, Pension Funds, etc.)	45–46%

Sourced from Commercial Bank Annual Reports, AMFI, Author's Calculations.
**Note: Commercial Bank holding of corporate debt is primarily for brokerage business (margin pledges), and rarely as collateral for Repo borrowings. RBI's new guidelines[128] now allow commercial banks to keep corporate debt (non-financial) as Held-to-Maturity (as part of non-SLR holdings). It remains to be seen how bank treasuries will evolve, and whether such securities see actual action at the LAF window (Repo/Reverse Repo/OMO) of the RBI. #Statutory Liquidity Ratio (SLR) mainly comprises GSecs and free cash.*

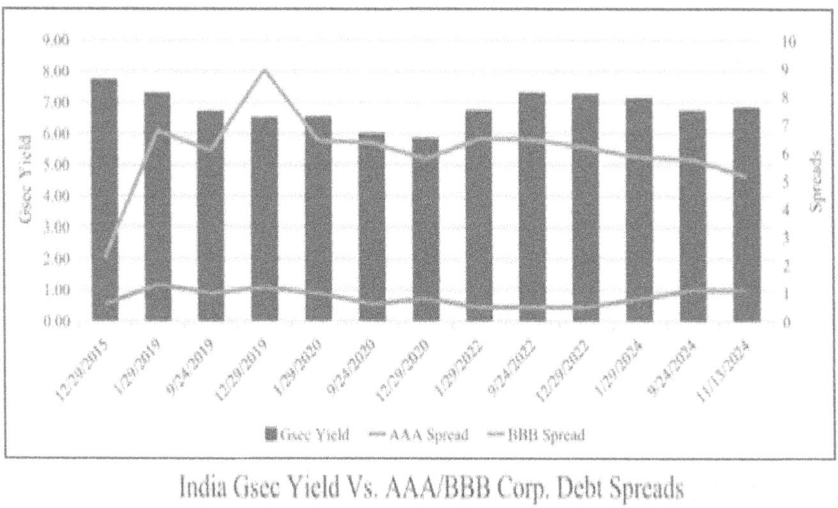

Figure 26: Depicting yield spreads of Indian AAA and BBB-rated corporate debt. Pre-post-COVID period evolution.

Sourced from the author's research based on market and corporate performances.

128 Business Standard: RBI decides to include corporate debt under HTM: https://www.business-standard.com/economy/news/rbi-decides-to-include-corporate-bond-under-held-to-maturity-category-123091301131_1.html

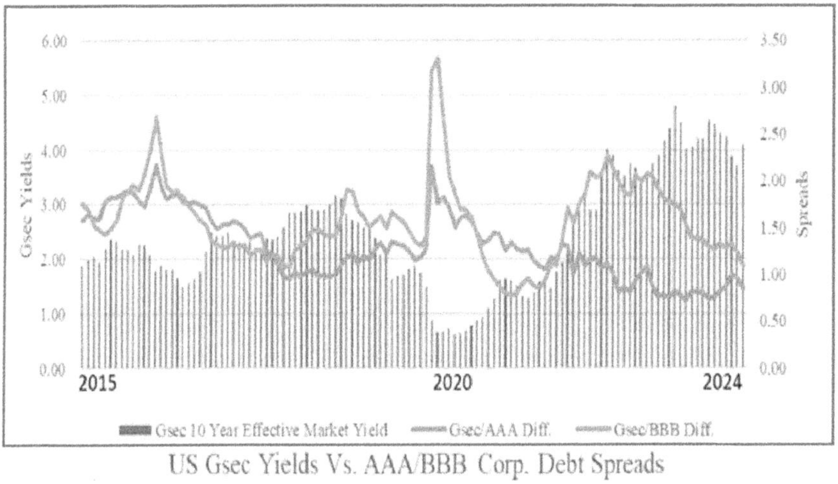

Figure 27: Spreads between US Government yields and US corporate debt (both AAA and BBB) yields. Duration normalized.

Sourced from Fred St. Louis; SIFMA. Chart: Karan Mehrishi.

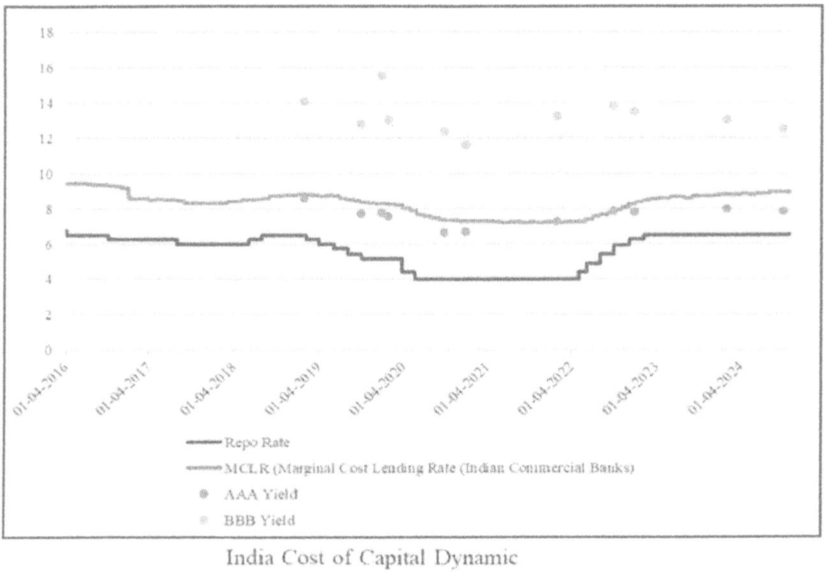

Figure 28: Depicting the cost of capital dynamics, comparing Indian corporate debt yields (AAA and BBB rated) with prevailing MCLR and Repo Rate.

Sourced from Macrobond, SEBI, NSDL Data. Chart: Karan Mehrishi.

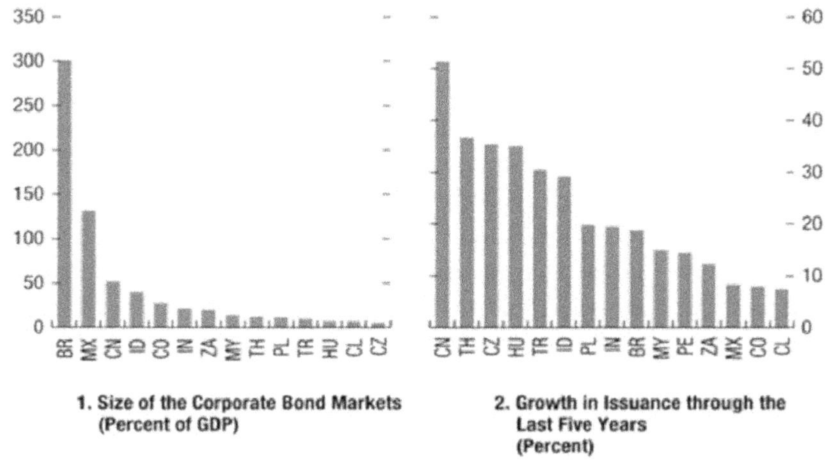

Figure 29: Depicting size and issuance growth of corporate debt.
Sourced from IMF Report: Corporate Debt Market: Evolution, Prospects, and Policy (Surti, Goel, 2023).

The LoLR Misnomer in the Indian Monetary System[129]

A Brief History of the LoLR Function in India

In the 1930s, Emergency withdrawals under the 'Statutory Deposits' facility in India were similar to Committed Liquidity Facility (CLFs) in the United States, proposed by BIS economist Bill Nelson. This facility was like an insurance policy for commercial banks, which were required to maintain 5% Demand Deposit, and 2% of Time Deposit equivalent with the RBI during normal times. The RBI allowed eligible commercial banks to withdraw these deposits during times of crisis. These deposits were defined in RBI parlance as 'Statutory Deposits', and were part of the second last liquidity access window for commercial banks at the time. The facility was empowered by Section 42 of the RBI Act, 1934.

Apart from 'Statutory Deposits', the RBI's primary Lender of Last Resort (LoLR) function, providing liquidity against eligible securities, as collateral

129 This is the author's original research, and part of his submitted coursework at Yale University.

(Explained under Section 17 of the RBI Act, 1934), remained a cornerstone of liquidity operations as a system back-stopper. The RBI could also choose to restructure banks, and often demanded the release of the provisional investigation report (as was done during the TNQ Banking Crisis in 1938).

In the current monetary operations pertaining to the RBI's LoLR function, the MSF under the LAF has emerged as the primary cornerstone. The SLR nevertheless offers insurance policies to banks in trouble, rather it merely offers collateralized loans (against eligible Government Securities) at a penal rate that is 25 bps over and above the prevailing Repo Rate. The trouble is that accessing the SLR facility forces banks to hold sufficient Government Securities at all times as part of their HQLA holdings, which is in turn part of the Basel 3 mandated Liquidity Coverage Ratio (LCR) calculations. This condition, however, invariably leads to a collateral constraint problem for commercial banks often most impacted are the smaller ones during a crisis.

A Brief History of the LoLR Function in the United States

Since the 1920s, the discount window (DW) has been highly regulated, so much so that it still evokes a sense of reluctance among commercial bankers in the United States, and this has resulted in the DW being associated with a stigma (that still exists today). While there is a moral hazard dilemma involved here, there are historic lessons that must be considered before reaching any judgements. Ultimately, this write-up's primary purpose is to present the thesis that the Fed's LoLR function (which is another name for the DW) is sacrosanct in maintaining the public's confidence in banking, and without such support, US banking will always operate in an environment of uncertainty. The constant comparison of the US Fed's LoLR function with the Moral Hazard problem is therefore not always right, as sometimes inherent banking business nuances must be considered as well.

The history of the LoLR is as important as the history of the Federal Reserve System itself, even though the term was arguably coined by Sir Francis Baring in 1797, as part of his observations on the establishment of the Bank of England. Nevertheless, in many ways, LoLR cannot be looked at in isolation and is intertwined with American central banking from the beginning and forms the very principles on which the Federal Reserve is based.

Therefore, in the American context, the genesis of the LoLR lies in the passing of the Aldrich-Vreeland Act in 1908 (Berstein et al., 2010), which allowed certain commercial banks to issue emergency liquidity to vulnerable banks when bank-run type situations threatened the entire system. Importantly, the Aldrich-Vreeland Act was passed in conjunction with the Federal Reserve Act in 1913, which established the Federal Reserve as a central banking entity within the United States.

What this means is that the idea of the LoLR even predates the Federal Reserve, and the latter can be termed as a formalized embodiment of the LoLR function.

This makes LoLR and the Federal Reserve inseparable, and the existence of one cannot be justified by the non-existence of the other. Therefore, with the establishment of the Federal Reserve System, the LoLR function was transferred to it, and the latter became synonymous with the 'Discount Window' (DW), which, in turn, comprises three types of emergency loans, namely: Seasonal, Primary, and Secondary. Nevertheless, it can be argued that DW is not necessarily the only true representation of the LoLR, but more on that later in this section.

While the LoLR was established to fight the vulnerabilities emanating from the seasonal nature of agriculture, post-World War 1, the function evolved, streamlining itself with changing circumstances. Consequently, the LoLR saw action in both liquidity as well as fundamentals-driven bank runs, and associated financial crises (Correia et al., 2024).

Historically, the most pivotal episodes that have defined the LoLR have been the following:

1. 1929–1933: The Great Depression and associated contractions.
2. 1970: Default of Pennsylvania Central Transportation Company (Penn Central)
3. 1987: The Stock Market Crash (Black Monday).
4. 2001: 9/11 Terrorist Attacks.
5. 2007–2009: The Great Financial Crisis (GFC).
6. 2023: Signature Bank & SVB Bank Runs

Remarkably, the Federal Reserve has finetuned its LoLR function (with the DW) based on the requirements of each economic event, and has introduced several initiatives to make the DW more flexible and accessible to the system (especially after the Dodd-Frank Act in 2010 that expanded the scope of LoLR (Scott, 2020). This is because all banking crises are characterized by certain nuances that require a customized approach. By virtue, there is really no one-size-fits-all approach here. While DW, which is known to be an emergency collateralized window, accepting loan assets as well as government securities domestically as collateral, the LoLR function itself has evolved, and expanded its scope (though still insisting on some form of collateral) with:

1. Committee on Uniform Securities Identification Procedure (CUSIP) Swaps (English, 2011)
2. Federal Reserve Act (Section 13 (3)) empowered the creation of an emergency window for money market, and insurance companies/funds (English, 2011).
3. Standing Repo Facilities (SRF), as a junior window to DW.
4. The Federal Reserve Act (Section 14) empowered Currency Swap Lines with select foreign central banks.
5. Bank Term Funding Program (BTFP), under Section 13 (3), for emergency loan provisions (Kelly, 2024).

Additionally, former Federal Reserve and BIS economist Bill Nelson proposes the establishment of Committed Liquidity Facilities (CLFs) as a prepaid add-on service that can be subscribed from the Federal Reserve by banks during normal times.

This brings us to Mark Carlson's thesis on the background objectives of the LoLR, which he divides into three components, namely:

1. Managing uncertainty regarding the liquidity and solvency of institutions at risk.
2. Incorporating flexibility and designing a focused approach for a problem.
3. Effective information flow management.

Based on these components, it can be argued that Carlson's contentions pertain to the historic balancing between 'moral hazard, and risk shifting', whenever the LoLR was utilized. In a way, this trade-off remains the core of the Federals Reserve's LoLR function. This understanding is also sacrosanct for commercial banks/financial institutions (borrowers) and the public at large, as the availability of the LoLR is not always a given.

This brings us to the point of 'stigma' that is associated with DW, and associated windows, as commercial bankers usually excuse themselves from it. Carlson himself explains the phenomenon in his paper, and notes that DW operations, 'resulted in losses, as well as public relation challenges for the Federal Reserve'. This happened, notes Carlson, because unsatisfactory resolution processes and excessive usage of DW by certain banks caused moral hazard problems. 'This caused Reserve Banks to tighten standards, making borrowers reluctant to borrow.'

Bill Nelson further notes that 'several times, the Federal Reserve has increased stigma to reduce borrowings, especially between the 1920s, and 1950s'. This has resulted in hesitancy among bankers to utilize the DW, even more so after the passing of the Dodd-Frank Act, 2010, post the GFC. While expanding the LoLR capacities, the act enforced several regulations (including but not limited to additional capital requirements) on bankers, and sought information on general banking (reporting requirements (Fischer, 2016) in the event of DW utilizations, and consequent identified irregularities.

The most recent usage of the DW in the US post the GFC, and COVID-19, happened during 2024 first half, when the SVB Bank faced bank runs, auguring imminent fallout on the entire American financial system.

Lessons for the RBI & Learnings from the US Fed's DW & CLFs post-COVID-19

Post-COVID-19, RBI weekly data suggests that smaller commercial banks did invariably scramble for liquidity, despite sufficient liquidity support from the RBI and excess systemic liquidity in general. This resulted in significant demand at the MSF window, and smaller banks may have faced collateral constraint problems invariably since Government Securities are eventually exhausted, and no other security can be utilized as collateral. This author is therefore convinced that the RBI must bring back 'Statutory Deposits' from Section 42 of the RBI Act into action, and make it a mainstay as a systemic liquidity support tool. This will be in line with the American CLFs and redefine the Indian central bank's LoLR function for good. The move will also absolve the RBI of any criticism pertaining to its inability to rescue individual banks during a crisis without the Moral Hazard problem.

In recent history, while the RBI has been a great liquidity facilitator at the system level, it has not been of much help at the bank level – solely dependent on the effectiveness of system liquidity support, and the access to the MSF window. This has to change for the better, alleviating the system from the collateral constraint problem, and allowing commercial banks to ensure their liquidity needs during a crisis by depositing requisite funds with the RBI during normal times. For starters, the CRR may be transformed into a redeemable account as it is anyway, non-interest-bearing, but this will evoke more debate that is outside the scope of this book project.

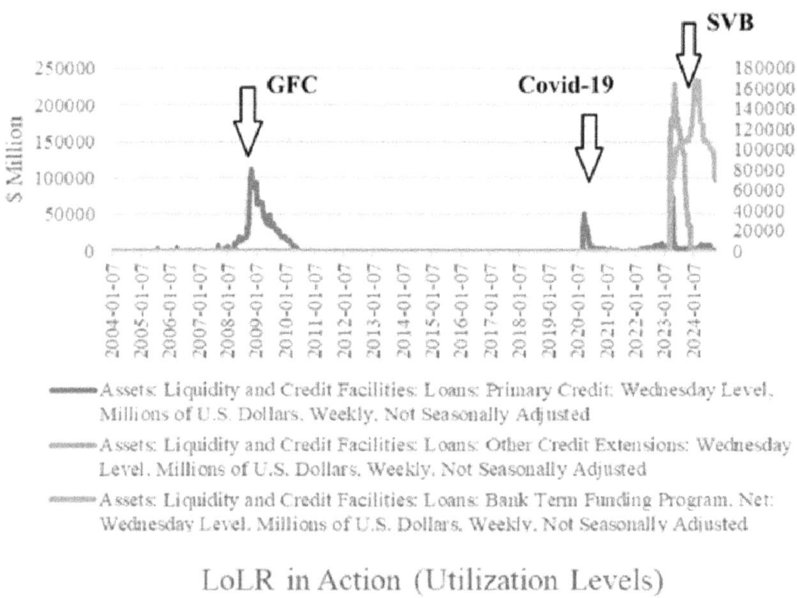

Figure 30: Depicting the prevailing Discount Rate as compared to the quantum of loans to commercial banks.

Sourced from Macrobond; Federal Reserve System Data. Chart: Karan Mehrishi.

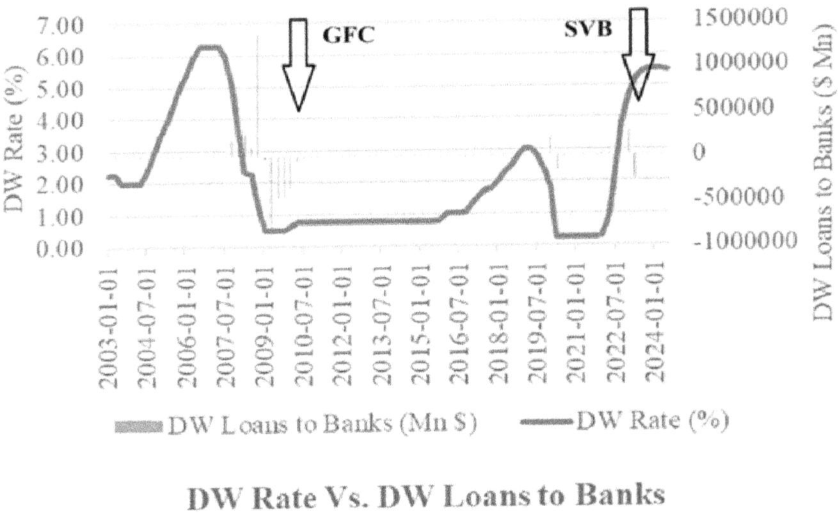

Figure 31: Depicting Federal Reserve DW utilizations during crisis periods.
Sourced from Macrobond; Federal Reserve System Data. Chart: Karan Mehrishi.

Government of India's Policy Misses & Adverse Socio-Economic Cascading Effects

Moral Hazard 1: Ignoring Household Stresses

The author believes that complete COVID-related lockdowns were a mistake as the unplanned move permanently destroyed productive capacities in different sectors of the economy. Despite the dissatisfaction, there are other concerns too that deserve more attention, and one of these includes the ignorance of household stress levels.

The fact of the matter is that the Indian Government failed to provide 'consumption/bailout packages' for middle-income households, at any time during the crisis. This could have been achieved through subsidies and related incentives for consumers. While this could have lowered the government's indirect tax collection, the resultant consumption could have compensated the exchequer for the revenue foregone.

For much of the COVID-related financial crises, public capex for economic sustainability is perhaps the only game in town. As per data from the MOSPI, the proportion of Government Final Consumption Expenditure (GFCE) in nominal GDP was pegged at 12.5 per cent in the Financial Year 2021.

This was a full 130 bps expansion, as compared to the previous year. The reason pertains to the fact that, in the backdrop of consumption falling during the initial phases of the pandemic, the private sector abstained from capacity expansion, as the priority was business continuity.

With the lockdowns implemented by the Government of India in a bid to safeguard lives, the economy contracted by over 20 per cent in the first quarter of the Financial Year 2021. While the Government succeeded in its endeavour (to an extent), the overall contraction (in real terms) was a little over 7.2 per cent for the year, and significant capacities were lost. Therefore, inherent weaknesses in the economy became visible, and private consumption, which is the backbone of the Indian economy, started to contract.

So much so that core services (including hotels, trade, and transport) contracted by a significant 18.2 per cent, in real terms. The bigger news at the time was that the share of private household consumption, as a proportion of GDP, declined to 58.6 per cent, from the previous year's 60.5 per cent, in nominal terms. It has been very few times in India's economic history that such circumstances have become apparent. The agriculture sector, on the other hand, continued to expand in its historic range of 3–4 per cent, but this performance was not sufficient to keep rural household demand at sustainable levels.

The lingering effects of this economic reality were apparent even in the status presented by the FY2024 numbers, as consumption has contracted even further in real terms, as a percentage of GDP. In real terms, real household consumption (unadjusted for inflation) as a proportion of GDP is now just 55.6 per cent in FY2024. This is astonishing because even during the COVID-related lockdown for much of FY2021, the proportion of household consumption was 56 per cent.

Household debt levels are also high, and denote the fact that households are finding it difficult to stay afloat amidst a high-interest rate environment and obstinate inflation. A look at the over 20 per cent consistent growth in the non-collateralized (personal loan) loans category gives us a sense of the debt trap households are increasingly finding themselves in, even today. At this time, we must take a step back and analyse the problem.

The problem that one encounters while thinking in hindsight is that the priorities set by the Government of India during the 'planning for pandemic' phase were themselves oriented towards structurally securing the economy. In the hoopla, Indian policymakers almost completely forgot about the households per se, when globally, the latter were the epicentre of public dole-outs. The logic at the time was simple: a lockdown would force households to put a full stop to non-core consumption (of non-essentials), and the residual savings would carry Indians through. Since the Government would ensure safeguarding jobs through liquidity provisions from the RBI, households will remain in safe hands (somewhat). Not considering the plight of the poor households (primarily of daily wage earners), in a way, this strategy did work, given the fact that the massive liquidity avalanche caused a glut in the system, and was conveniently driven towards the capital markets by opportunist mutual funds.

Nevertheless, the overall consumption suffered, and massive inventories were created across the economy. This happened because the investment function overtook the consumption function (thanks to herd mentality and peer pressure), and financial market outperformance provided a semblance of overall prosperity in the economy.

Something that wasn't the case at all. FY2024 numbers reveal that per capita household consumption grew by just 2.1 per cent in real terms, when the overall economy is expected to grow by almost 7.6 per cent. The trouble is that this trend at the micro level has been ongoing ever since COVID-related macroeconomic turmoil ensued, and little attention is diverted in this direction. Private investment, and associated capex not meeting expectations, is perhaps the barometer policymakers must consider as they assess past policy mistakes.

It must be recalled that during 2020, when the pandemic-related disruptions were at their peak, the Government had borrowed an incremental ₹4.2 lac crore, post the announcement of the first bailout package. Part of this package was a component worth ₹1.6 lac crore, which was, at the time, was believed to be a dole-out fund for households under stress. Nevertheless, this was later distributed among centrally sponsored schemes – a move that this author believes was a missed opportunity and would have gone a long way as an experiment for direct transfer to stressed households.

Going ahead, since the Government will have limited capacity, it is high time that it allocates resources for the purpose of consumer subsidies. In a way, this should be treated as an act to correct the previous wrongs. The idea here is that household consumption must be revived to sustain the economy in the medium to long term. While it is true that this strategy will delay the FRBM alignment and encourage core inflationary tendencies momentarily, the resultant multiplier effect will be significant for improving sentiments in the economy.

Provisions for interest subvention schemes, especially for low, middle-income, and vulnerable households for the consumption of real estate, white goods, automobiles, other consumer durables, and importantly, for one-time settlements of bad loans – must become a priority.

This, in a way, will not provide a good precedent for future generations, engaged in exuberance, but then black swan events do not come often, and COVID-19 can surely be a historic exception. Policymakers can therefore potentially revive India's consumption story and help normalize consumption disparities with quick thinkingand envisioning innovative solutions in the near term.

It is possible that dividend payouts from public institutions can help in incremental tax accruals for the Government, potentially paring down some fiscal losses incurred previously; the current priority must be all about ensuring the churning of the virtuous cycles, and reinvigorating the economy's animal spirits. Capex-driven growth, as a proven formula for growth, is indeed a proven way to continue economic expansion; it is now becoming increasingly clear that there are limitations of the model, amidst the current realities.

Moral Hazard 2:The Pandora's Box Called Healthcare Inadequacies

India's century-old ignorance of the public healthcare system was exposed by the pandemic, and a macroeconomic response proved to be inadequate while dealing with the situation quickly. Policymakers must solve this policy quagmire as soon as possible, but first, the analysis.

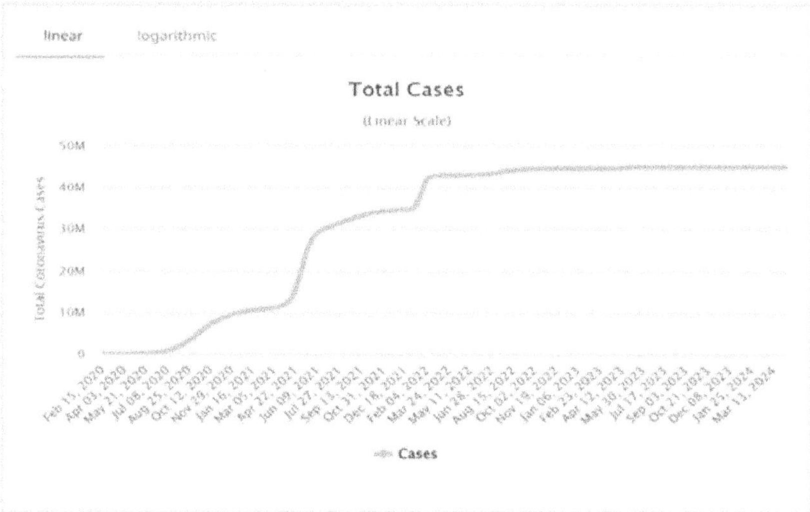

Total Coronavirus Cases in India

Figure 32: Depicting the Corona case load in India during the pandemic period.
Sourced from Worldometer[130] *Data & Chart.*

For India, COVID-19 opened a Pandora's box that lay hidden beneath piles of bureaucratic hurdles, lack of planning, and lack of vision of past leaderships. Towards the end of 2021 (until when 3–4 lockdowns, in varied phases, had already been initiated), India recorded over 32 million COVID cases and had already lost over 420,000 citizens.

Until 2024, the death toll was estimated to be anywhere between 500,000 and 600,000, but according to the WHO estimates, the number was likely at least several times higher than the official figure. In any case, the official numbers were, at the time, second only to the United States, where infection rates were rising rapidly among the diasporas. Amidst the blame game, while the Government officials, as well as associated policymakers, were busy pacifying the populace, human suffering across the country was excruciating, with no solution in sight.

130 Worldometer Data: https://www.worldometers.info/coronavirus/country/india/

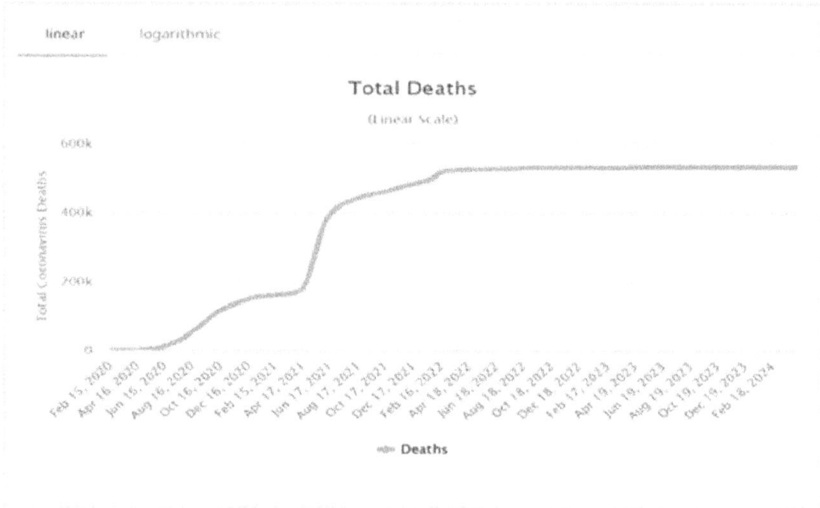

Total Coronavirus Deaths in India

Figure 33: Depicting human lives lost during the pandemic period.
Sourced from Worldometer[131] *Data & Chart.*

Endless lines of patients in desperate need of medical help, and unable to find hospital beds, showed a very sorry state of the Indian healthcare system, which deserves no excuses. Learning lessons quickly, it is about time for the policymakers to prepare the nation for any health-related disasters in the future and create necessary bulwarks. In a way, it is time to initiate a Health-proofing exercise across India, without losing any time.

It was apparent that the private sector was overwhelmed by the disaster and needed support from the Government, going ahead. As a solution, India should have invoked Article 352 of the Indian Constitution, which would have provided the Indian Government with financial and constitutional powers to address the inadequacies swiftly.

Deriving some fundamentals from the U.S War Powers Act, India should have strategically aligned Government departments and state functionaries towards the rapid creation of required capacities and core medical facilities.

131 Worldometer Data: https://www.worldometers.info/coronavirus/country/india/

Timely procurement of assets for the purpose of meeting these strategic goals could have also been considered. As a special exercise, the financing needs could have been then taken care of by 'purpose-built' capital market instruments.

India's primary healthcare system needs special focus, as data prove the existence of just over 30,000 such centres across the country. What this means is that there is not even 1 primary health centre for 10,000 Indians, at any given time! One reason for this anomaly is the existence of private healthcare practitioners, who take care of public needs, but the situation leads to a significant burden on household finances. Today, public healthcare expenditure, which is a combination of centre and state contributions, is a little over 1.4 per cent as a proportion of Indian GDP. Needless to say, this is one of the lowest health-related allocations among G20 nations.

Consequently, low public health beneficiary status forces households to utilize personal sources of finance during health-related adverse events, and bear roughly 60 per cent of medical expenses, out of their own pockets. To put things in perspective, the number for the United States is just around 50 per cent.

Furthermore, data from the World Bank suggests that 'India has just 0.5 beds for every 1000 people', for patients requiring serious medical care and hospitalization. Here again, to put things in perspective, China and Japan have around 4 and 13 beds, respectively. Perhaps, the time is right to correct historic mistakes and mollify public bitterness for good. As we plan for the future, policymakers must remain aware that while additional borrowings can potentially increase the country's indebtedness, the safety and security of India's future generations cannot be ignored.

Moral Hazard 3: Ignoring the Corporate Debt Market Liquidity

The COVID-19 pandemic-related crises exposed the non-acceptability of the corporate bond market in India as a reliable instrument of exchange within the country's financial system. The fact of the matter remains that the corporate bond market continued to remain without any special window at the RBI and was therefore exposed to the vagaries of the capital market, at its worst.

The crowding out effect from significant issuance of government debt also exacerbated the plight of private sector issuers during the pandemic era.

Looking back, the March 2020 redemption debacle is still a fresh memory, and will remain so, when the history of the evolution of India's fixed income/mutual fund is ever written.

An excerpt from this author's article: 'How Regulations Failed Our Fixed Income Market', *published as HT Mint Opinion, in HT Mint, on 6th October 2021*[132] *(Karan Mehrishi, 2021)*

> Amidst the denigration inflicted upon the industry, perhaps the greatest error of judgement pertained to the convenient omission of the fact that India lacks a credible secondary market for corporate debt securities. What this means is that the risk of holding such debt is extremely concentrated in the system, which in India largely comprises the RBI, commercial banks, FIIs and mutual funds.
>
> The events unfolded just as the COVID-19 crisis started to become a serious threat, spooking investors. As the global economy started to feel the heat, there were momentary capital outflows from emerging markets, leading to significant capital market volatility. Amidst falling interest rates, the understanding at the time was that global capital might find solace in safe-haven assets elsewhere.
>
> The ensuing panic led to redemptions to the tune of $26.3 billion (five-year high) in the month of March 2020 from debt-focused funds. Consequently, these pressures left relatively risky debt funds vulnerable as liquidity became an obstacle in meeting commitments. This was also because there was no interest in the secondary market for a significant quantum of corporate paper held by mutual funds, which often hold such instruments until maturity. Amidst drying out FII money, while the RBI had no specialized window dedicated to the industry, uncertain commercial banks excused themselves by way of their rising LCR obligations.
>
> Equalling 100%, the LCR is a short-term liquidity stress test and is a ratio of HQLA stock and 30-day net cash outflows. Ironically, while mutual funds are used as vehicles for exposure in corporate debt by banks, they are reluctant to hold such securities

132 HT Mint Opinion (Karan Mehrishi, 2021): https://www.livemint.com/opinion/online-views/how-regulations-have-failed-our-fixed-income-securities-market-11633536507546.html

directly. The sudden increases in key benchmark yield spreads made matters worse. The rest, as we know, is financial history.

RBI's consequent introduction of the $6.6 billion Special Liquidity Facility for Mutual Funds (SLF-MF) window was an admission to an earlier oversight. It was a realization that the industry's vulnerabilities cannot be ignored. The fact remains that over the years, the fixed-income mutual fund industry has emerged as an important financier of India's nearly $500 billion corporate debt securities market. Setting the context, debt-focused mutual funds collectively manage $212 billion in assets (as of August 2021). This is roughly 7% of the Indian GDP, when compared to 26% averaged by the mutual fund industries in the European Union and the United States.

Nevertheless, carrying more than its weight, India's mutual fund industry directly finances 43% of the country's corporate debt instruments. The global average among peers is just over 15%. Evidently, the mutual funds industry is possibly the only source of funding for a significant quantum of issued debt in the segment. These numbers become starker when one considers that for paper that is rated below AA (–), the secondary market essentially does not exist, at least in a T+1 settlement regime.

Oriented for decades through one of the world's highest statutory holding requirements, commercial banks have traditionally found safety only in government debt securities despite their pivotal role in the fixed income market. Once bitten by the NPA bug, banks have also become risk-averse and have emphasis on building their portfolios with the highest achievable ratings. On average, the proportion of government securities held by Indian banks is nearly 85% of their investment portfolios and over 21% of their total asset size. This is extraordinary as research by Gennaioli et al. has previously shown that the world average is just around 9% of assets and goes to around 11% in periods of crises. This causes a voluntary crowding out of non-government paper in India.

Perhaps a better understanding of this situation can be gained through a more detailed assessment of the HQLA stock, which has a significant overlap with the SLR guidelines. Since both SLR and HQLA Level 1 comprise of highest quality liquid assets, over 94% of such portfolios are made up of government securities. In fact, HQLA Level 1 stock not only includes government securities in excess of SLR but also equivalent SLR carve-outs such as MSF and Facility to Avail Liquidity for Liquidity Coverage Ratio (FALLCR). Level 2 HQLA, on the other hand, aims for diversification through lower rating requirements (>AA-) and is capped at 40% of the total HQLA stock. This cap is, however, never reached as NBFC/MFI-issued instruments are not acceptable as per regulations.

Theoretically, the higher the Level 1 stock, the healthier the LCR, since the segment attracts 0% risk weight under the Basal Committee on Banking Supervision (BCBS) guidelines. During the crisis, as commercial banks raced to safeguard their balance sheets, HQLA Level 2 received a further blow. This happened because certain banks chose to increase the share of FALLCR multifold at the cost of their Level 2 obligations. Consequently, major commercial banks nonchalantly increased their LCR significantly from 110% to 120% before the crisis to over 130% to date. The initial failure of LTRO 2.0 is a case in point, as banks were sceptical in parking their cash in corporate paper, fearing impact on LCR. The purpose of the HQLA Level 2 is to add diversity in the stock through an eclectic mix of securities. A lack of quota guidelines for corporate paper in the segment has, however, reduced the secondary market depth even further.

Resolution of the problem, therefore, necessitates a deepening of the secondary bond market. At the soonest, the RBI must open a window or a special purpose vehicle for direct purchase of corporate debt during times of crises on the lines of other structurally important central banks. Secondly, the RBI must enable corporate paper's acceptability among commercial banks, as this will help the tradability of such securities. This can be done by way of revisions in the HQLA stock calculation rules, requiring the inclusion of corporate debt at least at Level 2, with certain relaxations in credit rating requirements. Importantly, the HQLA regulations must not be open to interpretation, rather mandated at both levels. Recent events have shown the vulnerability of the fixed income segment, which has and will play an important role in building Indian capital market resilience. The darkest hour is conceivably the best time to prepare.

Moral Hazard 4: Lack of Credible Fiscal-Monetary Coordination

The RBI and the Government of India operated separately, and their co-ordination amidst the pandemic era emergency stimulus operations was vague and left much to be desired. Therefore, going forward, a fiscal-monetary co-ordination is the need of the hour. Fighting the COVID pandemic, India found itself amidst the most dreaded macroeconomic gridlocks, i.e., 'active fiscal and active monetary policies'.

This happened because the fiscal and the monetary sides functioned as stand-alone frameworks, without actually looking in the side-view mirror. While the sides did work within the Keynesian Macroeconomic Framework initially, later operations became more isolated in terms of actual impact on the economy. Given the background, policymakers must take note of the works of macroeconomist Momi Dahan, whose renowned 1998 paper, 'Fiscal Effects on Monetary Policy', discussed the effects of tightening monetary policy on a government's fiscal mathematics, especially the study of deficits.

Among other suggestions, Dahan shows that in the short term, rising interest rates not only raise the government's fiscal deficit by way of raising interest payment obligations but also impede its tax revenue amidst a fall in output. It must therefore become the Government's priority to institutionalize a 'Fiscal-Monetary Coordination Committee', the mandate of which should be to meet quarterly and discuss economic deficiencies in real-time.

The idea here is that there should be an institutional set-up to discuss the Indian central bank's reserve and currency operations, as well as the government's expenditure planning. For this reason, this author suggests that Section 45Y of the RBI Act must be revised at the earliest, and fiscal and monetary sides must come to the table, as part of a well-thought-out macroeconomic policy. This should basically come as a learning for policymakers that the 'silo approach' is no longer viable in the modern era of institutional coordination.

CHAPTER 9

A Brief Discussion on Utilized Mathematical Models

The COVID-19 pandemic has changed the economics profession once and for all. Thanks to the American influence on modern economics, while the '*mathification*' of the subject has been an ongoing phenomenon – taking over almost all realms in the field, the pandemic sped up the process.

What has changed due to COVID-19 has been the rapid proliferation of the approaches followed by mathematical physicists, computing engineers, especially signalling and processing, into larger mainstream macroeconomics. Perhaps the initiator of sorts has been the uncertainty itself, given the non-availability of high-frequency data, and the resultant policy paralysis.

The problem was even more pronounced in developing countries such as India, where macroeconomists had to quickly hypothesize tools to assess the state of the economy in real time, without relying too much on quarterly, monthly, or even annual data releases.

Consequently, State Space Framework-based tools, automated with AR machine learning models, emerged as the go-to solutions during the COVID-19 era. In the following pages, an attempt has been made to briefly touch upon State Space framework approach, using the Kalman Filter (KL) as well as Hamilton Filter (HL) based Markov Switching framework, that were most prominent in high frequency data modelling among Indian economists (RBI SPF panellists included), as well as the RBI economic research teams. Given India's own data-related inadequacies, these approaches were also excessively utilized by Indian macro model builders across the industry.

We will now analyse these two most popular approaches, using, State-Space Models (using KL), while also touching upon Dynamic Factor Markov-Switching Modelling (DFMS), using HL. While the following chapter may appear to be a mathematical deviation given this book's intent to assess India's macroeconomic response to a crisis, this author feels that merely giving model results will be half-baked information. Also, given the importance of these emerging mathematical approaches and their relevance in this context, it was felt that an introductory dissection of the mathematics would provide a solid background to the readers before attempting to delve into the model outputs for India.

Kalman Filter & State Space Models

A State Space Example

$$\begin{pmatrix} n_t \\ x_t \\ x_{t-1} \\ Y_t \end{pmatrix} = \begin{pmatrix} 1 & 0 & 1 & 0 \\ 0 & 1 & 0 & 0 \\ 1 & 0 & 1 & 0 \\ 0 & 1 & 1 & 0 \end{pmatrix} * \begin{pmatrix} n_{t-1} \\ x_{t-1} \\ x_{t-2} \\ Y_{t-1} \end{pmatrix} + \begin{pmatrix} v_t \\ e_t \\ w_t \\ 0 \end{pmatrix}$$

Where:

Matrix is 4*4, and the output is a function of its own lags and error terms.

In the current context, State Space models can be understood as having the flexibility to assess a specific macroeconomic situation through multiple points of view.

A Simple State Space

Y = Transition Matrix * Lags + Error Terms

Followed by

Output = [Gamma/ Transition Matrix] * [Common Factor (F)]

Also,

Observables = [Matrix] * [Non-Observables] + [Shocks (in case there are error terms)]

The vectors within the designed state space represent the different points of view to assess an output (which we can assume to be GDP, for example).

Each vector consists of the variable used to calculate the output. What that means is that a single vector may be inhabited with Income, Employment, Production, or Inflation variables.

Once this is identified, a vector for each approach is built, and the model is trained by tracking past outputs, with past inputs (as posteriors).

While the autoregressive model is running the combinations with respective lags and priors, a Common Factor (F) is attained. This F then becomes the unobserved variable. The consequent co-movements among the combinations are recorded in the 'H Matrix', which, in turn, is represented by the elements:

$$\in (0,1)$$

If co-movements are encountered, the element 1 in the Matrix H is observed; if not, then a null space. The Gamma variables inhabiting the first column of the Matrix represent the Beta or the relationship of the variables used with the output.

Any portion of the co-movement that is not represented by the discovered common factor is represented by the 'error terms/ noise'.

These error terms are themselves run several times with their respective lags/priors, and the entire co-movement, along with those of the used variables, is represented in the 'Matrix F', which is a much larger Matrix pool.

Once this is done than the new state space representation is created where the Output (Y), which is trained from previous outputs, becomes a function of:

∫ [Common Factor (F) * Matrix H + Error Term]

Since the Matrix H consists of Elements (Gamma, 1, 0), the equation so achieved consists of combinations of Common Factor with Gamma, common factor with 1, and common factor with null spaces.

This is then added to the error terms.

Output (Y) = F*Beta + F*1+ F*0 + Error Term

Solving for the Matrix.

This then becomes the Kalman Gain. By character, the Kalman Gain adds more weight to the co-movements of the most recent data points, which means the weight assigned to t & t-1 will be higher than the weight assigned to t-1 & t-2.

After running several combinations (while training the model, which the Kalman Filter does automatically) of these vectors. A vector of vectors is achieved, representing the Common Factor of Common Factors.

This derived Common Factor finally becomes our 'Tracker' for the Output estimation.

Apart from the final output, the trained vectors representing different points of view can also be used to estimate the output of their used variables (through the level identified for that approach).

For example, the vector representing the 'Consumption' point of view to calculate GDP can be used to estimate IIP, since IIP is one of the variables used in this approach.

The vector is already trained and can estimate an output in real time.

It is important to remember here that a common factor of common factors represents all vectors after running the dynamic (using an AR (in most cases by further 2) model) in the following format:

Output (Y) = F*Beta + F*1+ F*0 + Error Term

Also, remember that using the level makes the model non-stationary (which is somewhat antithetical to the general perception that a GDP forecasting model must be stationary by nature).

It may be argued here that since the model is measuring the stationarity of the used variables (within the H Matrix), the error terms may remain non-stationary.

These error terms are ultimately an important component apart from the level of a real-time output. So, in a broader scheme of things, the final State Space equation represents both stationarity, as well a non-stationarity.

Furthermore, if we use a four-point-of-view model (in this case, for the forecast of the GDP), each vector would represent each point of view and contain those associated variables.

For all sense and purposes, the ultimate objective of the state space equation is to estimate the GDP (in this case). Therefore, the final equation will have the Common Factor (F) of Common Factors, which is the factor used to forecast the actual output (of t+1).

So, if we are estimating a monthly GDP, then the forecasted data point will be a function of the 'current months' level, which is generated on the monthly data available for the 'current month'.

Since the model is trained on the previous data points and previous outputs, the model estimates the required output based on the prior co-movements. This required output/estimated value is, of course, based on the level generated for the required month (the month for which the forecast is required).

The common factor generation for each month is thus the key to the model for forecasting.

The best-fitting models are those which have an MSE around 1 (or less than 1) and contain at least 1 weekly variable, and 3–4 monthly variables (as described by economist, Gabriel Perez-Quiros).[133] This can then be used to assess monthly variables.

MSE shows us how well a model has worked, and the model's efficiency is best when the MSE is closer to 1.

In general terms, small-scale models consist of a few variables (maybe 3–4), and large-scale models use a large set of variables (maybe more than 10). Therefore, while building the model, it must be considered that while increasing the dimension of the model than we are fundamentally adding more noise into the model, which, in turn, may represent unwanted correlations.

133 GEA Tracker: A Daily Indicator of Global Economic Activity (Journal of International Money and Finance: Elena Maria Diaz, and Gabriel Parex-Quiros, 2021) https://www.sciencedirect.com/science/article/abs/pii/S0261560621000498

When 'N' goes to infinity, the proportion of variances playing with the common factor decreases, and the variances of the level itself increase. And, therefore, the resultant common factor is less and less representative of what is happening in the overall economy.

This happens because shocks (error terms) become highly correlated to each other, as well as variable co-movement also represents high correlation – this, in turn, lowers the authenticity of the Common Factor (F) so derived, to predict outcomes. This is precisely why you must have a smaller scale model instead of a very large-scale estimation model. Remember, cross-correlation among variables and shocks is bad for the model and creates biased results. Therefore, while creating the vectors, one must consider this aspect, and include low-correlated input variables (to inhabit the vector).

Additionally, during the conversion of monthly data or quarterly data, the error terms are also assigned weightage, and therefore, the model will generate a level for these terms as well.

This interaction will be represented in Matrix F, and is done to make the monthly data that has been estimated by the model, and convert it to Quarterly data. This conversion to quarterly data involves the weightage of monthly data and the weightage of error terms.

Therefore, the estimated common factor (which is used to estimate the output) will then be a combination of the levels of both these components (Input variables and error terms). The fact of the matter is that when Error Terms are not weighted and left to themselves, they will be the stationary part of the model (within the state space universe of our model), and this will result in the interactions within the input variables to become non-stationary.

The recommendation here is to use weekly data to estimate the monthly data, and then a weightage of which can be used to assess the quarterly data.

Fundamentally, the basic difference between nowcasting through Principal Component Analysis (PCA Nowcasting) and Kalman is that the former only estimates output by measuring the variances in error terms, while not being concerned about the levels so generated.

On the other hand, the Kalman approach focuses on estimating an output based on a derived common factor, along with the variances in the error term (during the training phase). The similarity here is that both these approaches are 'continuous moving averages' models (as they smooth data by first estimating the mean (of co-variances) and then subtracting it from the variances). This, in turn, also helps us in ascertaining the co-movements among variables (and their lags) as shown in the transition matrix (H).

Given this condition, the model builders suggest that the variables must be as non-linear and time-varying as possible, because that is the best case for maximum co-movements (random), and this randomness is good to assess a realistic level. In other words, the more the noise, the better.

In the Bayesian approach, we assume from the beginning that the Coefficient (Gamma) and Sigma Square are random variables.

Understanding Model Workings

1. In the State Space Model, the Y_t is defined as what is defined as a desirable output. In other words, what is the output that the model has set out to achieve (in this case, Y_t, is the future Output or GDP). For that to be achieved, all previous Z_{ts} (measurements, which are basically based on 'actual' past outputs) are incorporated in the vector (as a learning vector), to figure out an unobservable factor (which can be defined as the common factor). This then becomes an estimator of future GDP/ new Y_t.
2. The measurements (past actual Y_{ts}), are defined in the Measurement Equation. These previous actual Y_{ts}, help in assessing the Z_{ts}. The machine learning tool delivers a new Z_t, based on its learnings from previous Y_{ts}, as a function of observed and unobserved variables (based on input variable co-movements).
3. Previous measurements, and their fit to the estimator model, are in turn assessed via the MSE.
4. The desired output, the new Y_t, is also defined as the new/desired system state.
5. Remember, every new level (which is unobserved part of the function) derived as part of a new vector (representing a new state space/system state equation) is assessed via the co-movements of the input variables, and how far (variance) these co-movements are from the mean (of all other co-movements) in the entire state space. The MSE is a good measure

of this, as it tells us the good fit of a function and its input variables to figure out a desired output.

6. The Optimal Output is the new Y_t, and the Z_t is the observed Output (Based on actual GDP data). Therefore, Yt is the 'predicted value', and the Z_t is the 'actual GDP value' (data of which is provided by government statistical offices). So, during the learning/training phase, we use Z_{ts} as previous outputs to determine Coefficients, and common factors, as a function of certain input variables.
7. When the dynamic reaches the penultimate stage, when an estimated output has to be provided by the model, the newest system state equation/vector will derive a Z_t (based on past Z_{ts}). Importantly, at this stage, no actual Output/GDP data is supplied, as we are no longer in the training stage. The derived Z_t is then 'Optimized' by multiplying with the derived Kalman Gain (which is basically the Common Factor of Common Factors), and adding to the 'previous actual GDP' figure supplied by the Government's statistics office.
8. The System State is defined as:

Y_t = Actual Previous GDP + Common Factor (F) * (Observed Z_t – Previously Observed Z_t)

We can say that the 'Optimal Output', which is in fact the final output at time t, is based on previous outputs (Z_{ts}), and actual GDP data supplied by the statistics office. This is defined by taking into account the Kalman Gain.

Dynamic Factor Markov-Switching Models (DFMS)

The Understanding

The Markov Switching (Hamilton Filter (HL)) is yet another approach used in real-time modelling of macros, and has emerged in assessing the state of the economy during crises.

During COVID, in the absence of high-frequency data, economists found themselves in a policy abyss, unable to navigate the dark waters of uncertainty.

As explained earlier, since India is a data-deficient economy, daily or weekly trackers were not available, and policy choices were at best following 'trial and error'.

For tackling such a difficult policy environment, the Markov Switching (using Hamilton Filter) has proved to be highly effective – providing policymakers dependable markers, assessing the economy's state in real time.

Perhaps the best way to understand the approach is to look at it from a continuous AR model, which learns as it grows. Just like an artificial intelligence tool, the model becomes better at assessment, as it is exposed to more data (or a sufficiently long running time series, which is, of course, optimized for black swan events, such as the COVID-19 pandemic).

A significant amount of work in the field of DFMS has already been done by renowned econometricians such as James H. Stock, Mark W. Watson,[134] S. Boragan Aruoba, Chiara Scotti, and Francis X. Diebold,[135] as well as Gabriel Perez-Quiros, Maximo Camacho, and Pilar Poncela,[136] among others.

The approach starts by first defining the possible states in which the economy:

1. **State 1 = Recession**
2. **State 2 = Not in Recession (Proxy for all other non-recessionary states)**
3. **State 3 = Transition from State 1 to State 2**
4. **State 4 = Transition from State 2 to State 1**

134 Estimating Turning Points Unsing Large Data Sets (Elsevier) https://www.sciencedirect.com/science/article/abs/pii/S030440761300198X

135 Real-Time Measurement of Business Conditions (IDEAS) https://www.researchgate.net/publication/228272358_Real-Time_Measurement_of_Business_Conditions

136 Dynamic Factor Markov-Switching Models in Real Time (Elsevier) https://www.sciencedirect.com/science/article/abs/pii/S0169207018300773

Imagine that we are trying to decipher whether our economy is in State 1 (Recession), State 2 (Non-Recession), or in transition.

While we define the output as Y_t, as the deciphering variable, it is important to remember that this is not the 'System State Output', that we seek.

To explain this further, let's consider a single variate model, where we are just taking GDP data as an input (because GDP is not Y_t, it is merely an Input Variable in this model).

Nevertheless, in a multivariate model, we can use GDP, IIP, and Core Industries as well. Therefore, the Co-movements by the running of the autoregressive (AR) model will be considered GDP_t, and GDP_{t-1}, (as posteriors) while figuring out Transition Probabilities, for example.

The Level (to assess h_t) will also be calculated like this. Fundamentally, this is the approach's primary difference from a Kalman Filter (KL) Filter as KL considers GDP as the Y_t, assessed via other Input Variables.

Very similar to the Kalman Filter Approach, here too, we consider a State Space, but this State Space consists of the above-mentioned two States (if we are considering a 2 State Model).

The System State Outputs in the State Space are therefore:

1. Probability of being in State 1 (S1)
2. Probability of being in State 2 (S2)

With this in the background, it is important to understand that the model doesn't know how to determine parameters (Constants, Gammas, Covariances, and Transition Probabilities).

In order to teach the algorithm, we must create 2 Density Functions (again, since we are considering a 2 State Model in the example):

1. Density Function_1 (Defining the Characteristics of State 1)
2. Density Function_2 (Defining the Characteristics of State 2)

The density function can be defined by the following function:

$$F(Y_t/\Omega_{t-1})$$

Where Ω_{t-1} representing the lags, is a posterior of Y_t

The Density Function is defined either by the modeller or tasked to the model to define under certain criteria. Once this is defined, the algorithm will then use these Density Functions as 'References' to define States, as it runs and learns (during its learning phase).

These Density Functions, in a way, can be defined as VARs, and therefore, in our case, become:

1. VAR_a
2. VAR_b

Which in turn can be associated with a Null Hypothesis – defined as H0, and H1.

In the learning phase, an AR model will run for Co-movements among input variables (for Y_t, which can be defined as GDP at a 'certain' State).

The resultant Single State Space will comprise:

State = (Transition Probability) *(Previous State) + Error Term

Therefore, the 'Previous State' is the 'non-observable' data point of the equation, and the 'Transition Probability', similar to the Transition Matrix, defines the 'Signals' achieved after running for Covariances.

This equation will give us the Probability of what to expect tomorrow (t+1, or time k), in the post learning phase.

The Previous States (h_t), are in turn defined/optimized by a Level (Common Factor). Here, the understanding is that if these Transition Probabilities return null spaces (0), then no signal has been achieved, and thus, there is no transition/switching to a different space.

In case there is 'p', or '1-q', it states that there is a case for Switching to a new State.

Taking reference from the defined 'Density Functions' (1 and 2), the algorithm will then define the Parameters for each new vector (which in turn is a combination of State 1 and State 2 parameters), and assign each vector to either State 1 or State 2.

Once the learning phase is complete, the algorithm will classify the new vector (in time k), either as State 1 or State 2, based on its previous learnings.

Therefore, throughout its running, the Markov Switching model will keep on Switching to either State 1 (which is subject to VAR_a), or State 2 (which is subject to VAR_b).

The algorithm will then consider the most recent data, considering it as 'Phase' in time t1. Based on the data assessed (most recent input data until that time), the algorithm will assign the 'Probabilities of being in each State'.

For example, in every 'Phase', the algorithm may assign 0.4 probability of being in State 1, and 0.7 probability of being in State 2.

In case it's a four-state model, then it may assign 0.4, 0.7, 0.1, and 0.3, respectively. This, in turn, can be defined as the probability of being in a certain 'State' at any given time. The highest probability (in this case, 0.7) is chosen as the likely State in that phase, under consideration.

Also remember, while assigning the 'Probabilities of being in a State' (which is the System State Output) during the defining phase (of the Density Functions 1&2), we can assign 0.5 (as output variable) to Density Function_1 and 0.5 (as output variable) to Density Function_2.

In case it's a four-state model, then we can assign 0.25 to each function. This is because the likelihood of occurrence for each State is 'equal'.

Another important fact here is the fact that all probabilities of being in States depend on or are subject to the previous or posteriors (in other words, data that precede the current State).

The Workings

In the HL approach, the non-observables follow a Markov-Switching Framework. Consequently, this approach is utilized for performing a Markov-Switching within a State Space framework.

1. $h_t = [\text{Prob}(S_1 = 1/\Omega_t]$
   $[\text{Prob}(S_2 = 1/\Omega_t]$
   $[\text{Prob}(S_t = \text{N}/\Omega_t]$

In Markov Switching (S_1), the Prob, and Prob (S_2), are two states/ points of view of the model.

These translate to (VAR_a), and (VAR_b). The dynamic will keep on switching to each VAR, with every new information introduced into the model.

S1 and S2 basically denote the States of the Economy. Generally, a 2 State model is utilized, but the use of a 4 State model is not very uncommon.

2. The objective of the Markov-Switching derivation is to Maximize the Likelihood Function, which, in turn, can be equated to the Density Function.

$$L = \sum_{t-1}^{t} ln\ F(Y_t / \Omega_{t-1})$$

Here, 'L' denotes the 'Maximum Likelihood Function', and Y_t (output) is subject to previous covariance.

Here Ω_{t-1} denotes previous observations (basically $Y_{t-1}, Y_{t-2}, X_{t-1}, X_{t-2}$...). Therefore, Y_t is subject to previous data of itself.
3. Value of the Probability in the Markov-Switching is derived by the Model.
4. The objective here is to figure out the Probability of being in each state in real time.

Nowcasting Model in Practice for India (Predicting COVID-19 Impact on Output)

Nowcasting Model for India can be designed as a simple exercise utilizing available high-frequency, and non-high-frequency macro data. The idea of the exercise is to demonstrate how accurate a carefully built nowcasting can be to forecast output, or any other variable, in real time. The way this works is that the model is fed with a time-series of 38 macro variables, including industrial output, inter-bank market, stock market returns, core industry sub-sector performance, and credit growth, among others. Since the model building is done in R, conditions 6 (year-on-year growth) and 0 (no growth) as a data frame are chosen for variable interaction.

Nowcasting is, as a matter of fact, a dynamic factor model (DFM), and therefore incorporates PCA, i.e., has factors that are in turn a combination of multiple variables that follow a specific trend. While this combination is random and is a model prerogative, it is safe to assume that the factors, or principal components, are a combination of specific variables that encompass a certain macro parameter, i.e., for example, IIP, Inflation, Financial Sector Performance, and Household Consumption.

Once the Factors are identified and created by the Nowcasting Model, the tool then assesses the historic 'estimated values' of the output (model output is GDP real growth at constant prices), and compares it with the historic 'actual values'. In case the model is based on a Kalman Filter approach (as elaborated earlier), the model then identifies common factors (level), and then outputs a forecast in real time for impending time periods (depending on the modeller's choice). Kalman Smoothening is used to further fine-tune the forecast. The Nowcasting Model that is being built here for India has the following parameters and demonstrates a highly accurate forecast, denoting minimal error when checking the model's effectiveness during the COVID-19 era, with no knowledge of what was, or could happen the parameters proved robust. Consequently, in this case, the model only has access to previous time-series primarily (with only few variables offering current data in real time). Nevertheless, the caveat worth noting though, is that the higher the availability of high-frequency data, the better.

Table 30: Variables Considered.

Core CPI	Import	Repo
Food	Import (Manu)	GVA
Oil	Credit Growth	USD Exchange Rate
IIP	GST Collection	Euro Exchange Rate
Fuel	Corporate Net Revenue	PMI (M)
WPI(M)	MIBOR_OR	PMI (S)
WPI(A)	Yield India 10 Year Govt. Sec.	BSE (Return)
Export	CM	
Export (Manu)	T-bill Yields	

Based on the author's considerations.

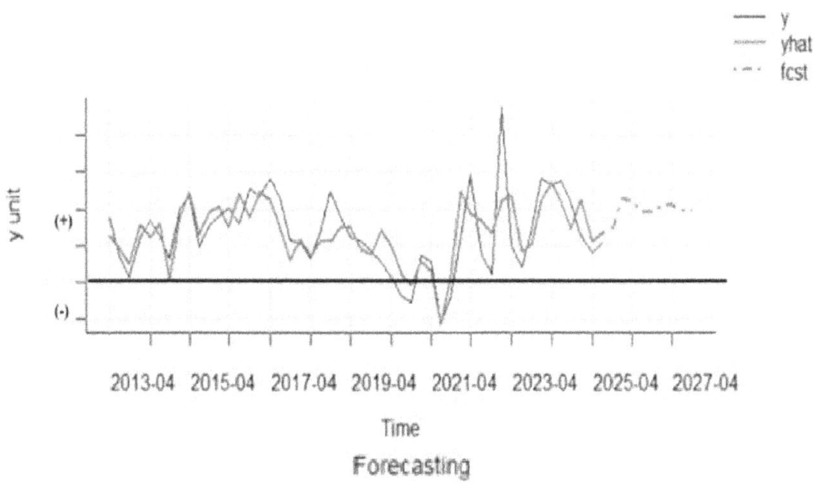

Figure 34: Depicting the model's forecast accuracy during the pandemic.

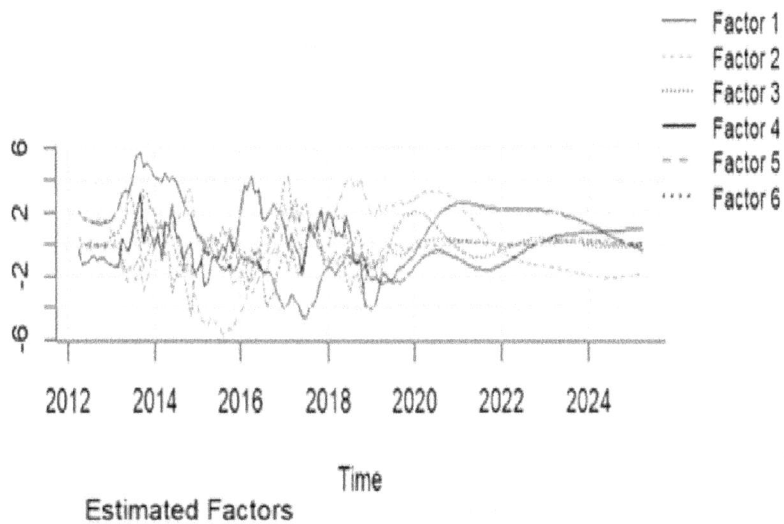

Figure 35: Depicting estimated factor evolution based on model output.

Table 31: Identified Factors (f) (Part of PCA)

Credit Demand
Economic Performance
Inflation
Industrial Performance
Trade
Exchange Rate
Financial Sector Performance

Kant et al.[137] of the Dutch Central Bank (DNB) define Nowcasting as 'predicting GDP of the past, present, and future'. What that means is that Nowcasting, as a forecasting technique, depends not only on actual data from the past but also the current data. Based on the model's own estimates for the time series, the future (forecast) is predicted.

Based on the works of Giannone et al.[138] a DFM-based Nowcasting Model can be created with a 'Two-Stage' Approach (Valk et al.).

The general specification can be defined as:

Defining Vector X_t *comprising of* $x_{1.t}, x_{2.t}, x_{3.t} \ldots x_{N.t}$ time series
Therefore, $X_t = P \cdot f_t + \varepsilon_t$

With P as a Parameter for Unobserved Factors (f_t), which in turn is based on the model's principal component selections.

X_t *is loaded to* f_t *via Matrice P* (representing signals emanated from both sides of the equation – this could be binary).

The data in the Vector can be transformed into quarterly data (for Quarter Q) with the following approach:[139] X_t = 3Q-2, 3Q-1,3Q

137 Nowcasting GDP Using Machine Learning Methods (DNB: Kant et al., 2022) https://www.dnb.nl/media/kq4pe4cr/working_paper_no_754.pdf

138 Nowcasting: The Real-Time Informational Content of Macroeconomic Data (Elsevier: Giannone et al., 2008) https://www.sciencedirect.com/science/article/pii/S0304393208000652

139 Nowcasting: The Real-Time Informational Content of Macroeconomic Data (Elsevier: Giannone et al., 2008) https://www.sciencedirect.com/science/article/pii/S0304393208000652

The common factors, in turn, are defined as:

$$f_t = \sum_{i=1}^{Pr} Ai\, f_{t-1} + Bu_t$$

Where $u_t \sim i.i.d.N(0, i_q)$[140]

Where q represents shocks.

Ai and B representing the matrices (measuring signals in the state space), and u_t *representing unobserved variables.*

The DFM states the condition that ε_t *(error terms) are mutually uncorrelated,* which means that $E[\varepsilon_{i.t}, \varepsilon_{j.s}] = 0$, for $i \neq j$.

As per Valk et al.[141] error term is modelled as an Auto-Regression (AR) process for period Pr.

A 2-period 2-factor (any two determined from the variables fed into the model) state space is then defined by Valk et al.

Again, referring to Giannone et al., Valk et al. then define the two stages as:

Firstly, the parameters of Matrice P, and for f_t *state space* are estimated using the PCA methodology. The condition here is that Vector X_t must have no missing values.

In this stage, estimators P' *and* f_t' are then determined using an optimization function (Stock et al.[142]).

In the second stage, the estimator for the variance/covariance matrices is then determined for the error term ε_t.[143]

140 Nowcasting: An R Package for Predicting Economic Variables Using DFM (R Contributing Research Article) https://journal.r-project.org/archive/2019/RJ-2019-020/RJ-2019-020.pdf

141 Nowcasting: An R Package for Predicting Economic Variables Using DFM (R Contributing Research Article) https://journal.r-project.org/archive/2019/RJ-2019-020/RJ-2019-020.pdf

142 Dynamic Factor Models, Structural Vector Auto Regressions in Macroeconomics (Princeton: Stock & Watson, 2011) https://www.princeton.edu/~mwatson/papers/Stock_Watson_HOM_Vol2.pdf

143 Nowcasting: An R Package for Predicting Economic Variables Using DFM (R Contributing Research Article) https://journal.r-project.org/archive/2019/RJ-2019-020/RJ-2019-020.pdf

$$\theta = diag\left[\frac{1}{T}\sum_{t=1}^{T}(X'_t - P'f'_t)\right)(X'_t - P'f'_t)']$$

Where:

X'_t being standardized panel with no missing values.[144]

f'_t in turn becomes the principal component of the normalized panel.

θ being the estimator for the variance matrices for the error terms.

In **Figure 34**, the Nowcasting Model shows its prowess in estimating the GDP/Output in real time based on monthly data. *Y^* is the estimator of the model, and closely follows actual data, based on unobserved factors so identified by the tool (based on variables fed as part of the data frame). This is perhaps the most potent tool that was used to assess the actual situation faced by the economy, and recommend what kind of policy tools were to be utilized, even before quarterly, half-yearly data was made available.

In all likelihood, Nowcasting models (whether using the Kalman Filter smoothing or expectation maximization) indeed proved their mettle in reducing reaction times during a black-swan event such as COVID-19. Perhaps, in the next edition of the book, a comparison between the effectiveness of the tool in the Indian context (with limited high-frequency data availability) with that in the American context (with significant high-frequency data availability) can be explored as an extension of the current explanation.

144 Nowcasting: An R Package for Predicting Economic Variables Using DFM (R Contributing Research Article) https://journal.r-project.org/archive/2019/RJ-2019-020/RJ-2019-020.pdf

CHAPTER 10

COVID as a Human Tragedy: A Kaleidoscope of Emotions of COVID Administrators (A Cross-Country Perspective)

As an event, COVID-19 is often dehumanized and is looked at through the lens of economics, mathematics, medicine, and as a history lesson. This is not wrong, and to an extent, scientific aspects did help in demystifying the unknowns brought about by this black-swan event. In fact, the rest of this book itself comprises these aspects.

This author, nevertheless, believes that above all else, COVID-19 was a human tragedy, and without the human element, no analysis will ever do justice to the macro management of an event such as COVID-19.

With this thought, this author has dedicated this chapter to the human story of COVID-19 from the perspectives of common citizens, who by a curious twist of fate happened to be in public service. Since COVID-19 was a pandemic of global proportions, this author is of the opinion that perspectives from India will not be sufficient to justify the human story of suffering and resilience.

Consequently, this author is presenting a kaleidoscope of perspectives from five countries, including India, for a cross-country analysis of COVID-19 as a human-centric event, impacting lives on the ground.

In the following pages, the author therefore presents points of view from citizens of Indonesia, Mexico, Namibia, and Japan, and weaves a story of emotion that has nothing to do with numbers, politics, or economics.

The story starts in Mumbai, India, where this author resided when the pandemic hit and ravaged the public, as well as the economy. The scramble in the initial days pertained to the assessment of the event and the extent to which it would impact normal human life. The fear of large-scale proliferation of infection, and potential loss of human life, was met by immediate lockdowns that restricted individuals to their homes, and 'non-essential' businesses were forced to close for a period of 21 days. The initial assessment was, however, conservative, as lockdowns ultimately became a perennial affair, and no respite was in sight.

As lockdowns ensued, and life was interrupted indefinitely, India's migrant labour force was the first to be impacted, and faced with the dreaded choice to either wait for better days, or traverse back to its home states on foot – often a thousand miles away.

While this author was gainfully employed at the time, and was comfortably ensconced in one of Mumbai's affluent neighbourhoods, the sight of hungry and hapless migrants desperately trying to get home has been etched in his memory. Consequently, as an economist, this author's primary recommendation for the Indian Government pertained to direct cash transfers to households and temporary accommodations for the transitory labour force stuck in economic centres across the country. This, he passionately pushed through his writings and commentaries.

This was, nonetheless, a slow and tedious process, and in the initial days, insufficient to address the human suffering. The collapse of the social fabric, as inadequate hospital beds and poor infrastructure were unprepared to handle the deluge of the sick and the dead, added a different dimension, forcing much deeper thought when ruminating on the impact of COVID, in hindsight.

From the life experience perspective, this author has largely lived a relatively privileged, big-city-centric life, away from the struggles of most of his countrymen.

Naturally, past life experiences did not prepare this author to deal with the harshness and insecurities brought about by the pandemic and its impact on the general public.

While the author performed his responsibility through his economics journalism, commentaries, and economic research, adding to the public's understanding of the financial crises brought about by COVID-19, the overall impact of his contributions was rather limited.

His experiences largely dealt with interactions with the white colour knowledge workers, as well as minor interactions with those belonging to the unorganized sectors, aiding the 'privileged life' in India, for the upper and middle classes. In a way, this background makes the author ineligible to undertake a project of this magnitude, and simply presents a macroeconomic view based on available data, trends, and subsequent mathematical analysis.

This lack of depth forced this author into introspection, and while writing this book, as an economist, the awareness was always at the forefront. Therefore, as part of a natural process of derisking his work from being termed disconnected, lacking context, and human connection, this author sought experiences from elsewhere across the world to present a comprehensive understanding. The best possible solution was consequently found in interviewing global young professionals working in public institutions, performing their duties during the pandemic, and having a front-seat view of the crises unfolding.

The idea here is to get the perspectives of young administrators from across the world, and understand what and how they do what they do. When it comes to the understanding of COVID-19 management, this author felt that it is important to first understand the emotions that make young men and women, working at the forefront of policy making during a crisis, function effectively.

For the sake of this chapter, these individuals share their experiences as common citizens, representing their countries. Points of view are from their varied life experiences, and the author would like to augment these global opinions with his own limited view of the pandemic unfolding, and its management.

As the pandemic hit India, there was a lot of debate around the learnings from the experiences in other countries in Asia, and how common citizens dealt with the problems associated with it. The prospectives of Ambang Febriyanto, an Indonesian citizen, prove invaluable here, as he shares his own life experiences, until the COVID-19 pandemic unfolded in 2020, and the aftermath.

Ambang works with Indonesia's banking supervisor, Indonesian Financial Services Authority (OJK), and has played a key role in ensuring Indonesia's banking stability during the COVID-19 crisis. As part of his duties, he had to travel when the COVID-19 pandemic was ravaging lives, and this he did despite being a father to a young daughter and being the primary breadwinner of his family. This resilience comes from his life experiences, as someone who was born in a village in central Java in a lower-middle-class family.

'Life was that of struggles, but I was determined to break free', he says.

Several years before he joined Bank Indonesia, Ambang was dealing with a difficult choice pertaining to whether he could continue his studies at Indonesia's elite engineering school, Bandung. He says he travelled to a city near his village, despite financial hardships, to prepare for the entrance examination, and worked very hard to get into his dream school.

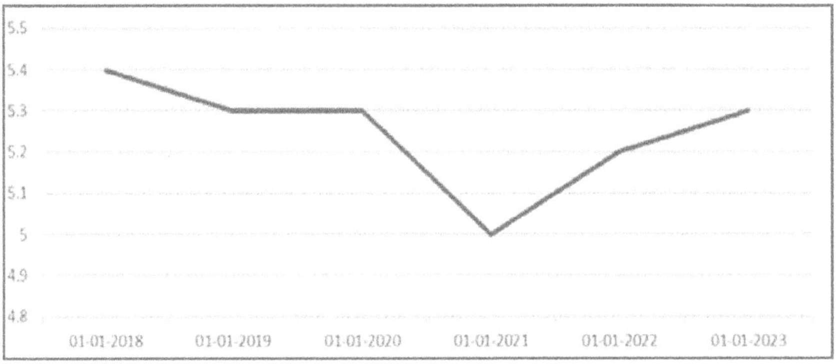

Indonesia GDP Growth (in Constant Prices) & Covid-19 Impact Minimal on Output

Figure 36: Depicting how the Indonesian economy fared during the pandemic period.

Sourced from Macrobond Data. Chart: Karan Mehrishi.

But as luck would have it, less than one semester into the program, his father lost his job, and financial troubles forced him to withdraw. Joining a Ministry of Finance-sponsored school instead, Ambang's next target was to join the bureaucracy, and he did everything in his power to get grades that qualified him to maintain his place at the school. Ambang says that he 'was among 2 per cent students in his country who actually made it through'.

Post graduation, Ambang joined the Ministry of Finance in 2009, and then the Bank Indonesia in 2011, in bank supervision, and chose to be part of the OJK in 2015, when supervision was separated from the former. Ever since, Ambang has been part of the OJK, and defines his career as eventful and, importantly, fruitful. When the COVID-19 pandemic finally hit, Ambang received his promotion and had developed expertise as a bank supervisor.

During the crisis, Ambang witnessed firsthand the impact on the economy unfolding, and how restructurings and accommodations helped save businesses that would have gone bust in case no help arrived.

Even though Ambang is of the view that enough was done in support of the households, he sees perception problems, as well as resource centralization, as key problems during the crisis. Ambang calls his wife the reason for his resilience as a professional, and simply says,

'She has always made me better'.

When asked about how scared he was about functioning as a professional in public service during COVID-19 on a scale of 1–10, he says, '6', because he knew his job was critical for his nation, and that 'things were under control'.

Ambang says that when he reminisces about his struggles, while sitting in his seventh-floor office, overlooking beautiful Jakarta architecture, 'I become grateful to the opportunities I have had, and what I do as a professional'.

Angga N. Pradana, another Indonesian national working for the Bank Indonesia as an economist, offers life experiences distinct from those of Ambang Febriyanto. Angga was born to affluent parents in the city of Surabaya, where his father was a senior banker. Having a great influence on his life and later career choices, Angga's father often travelled on business trips to assess local economies as part of his professional commitments.

He says that he used to travel with his father on some of these trips, and learnt a lot about Indonesia's economy and competitive advantages. This not only made him aware of his country's potential, but also gave Angga a sense of who he was, in terms of his nationality, as an Indonesian.

These experiences led him to choose economics as a worthy academic pursuit, attending the prestigious University of Indonesia in Jakarta for a Bachelor's degree in Economics. Angga says that 'There are many ways to serve public service but economics could address many aspects in society'.

Post his undergraduate education in economics, Angga briefly worked with a commercial bank honing his skills as an economist and market analyst. His sights were, however, set on the Bank Indonesia, and he was slowly moving towards his dream of working on the monetary side.

As if he had prepared himself for challenges, within a year of joining the Indonesian central bank, Angga was transferred to Papua province, which is traditionally underdeveloped, as compared to the rest of the country. This transfer was during the COVID-19's onset, sometime in 2020. Angga's brief was to understand the nuances of the inflation dynamics in the province, and knowledge sharing with the provincial staff of Bank Indonesia.

Angga's transfer couldn't have come at a more pivotal time, as COVID-19 made life difficult for common citizens, and by choosing to remain committed to his new, yet challenging posting during the pandemic, Angga demonstrated his resolve to play an important role in his country's resilience.

Interestingly, his wife is a qualified medical doctor, and her experience and knowledge helped Angga with the understanding of the pandemic and how it should be managed from the policy angle. Throughout his three-year tenure with the Papua provincial office, Angga performed his duties without flinching an eye and performed his duties with aplomb.

He says his learnings come from failures, setbacks, and this cycle keeps him learning, helping him continuously evolve himself, as a public services professional.

Shifting our attention to the Americas, Aitana González Alonso is a law professional working in the public services in Mexico. Like Angga N. Pradana, she also comes from a privileged background and went to a German bilingual school in Mexico City.

After attending the elite Mexican university for social sciences, Instituto Tecnológico Autónomo de México (ITAM) for twin bachelor's degrees in Political Science and Law, Aitana made the decision to enter public service on the recommendation of a professor, who liked her unique thought process.

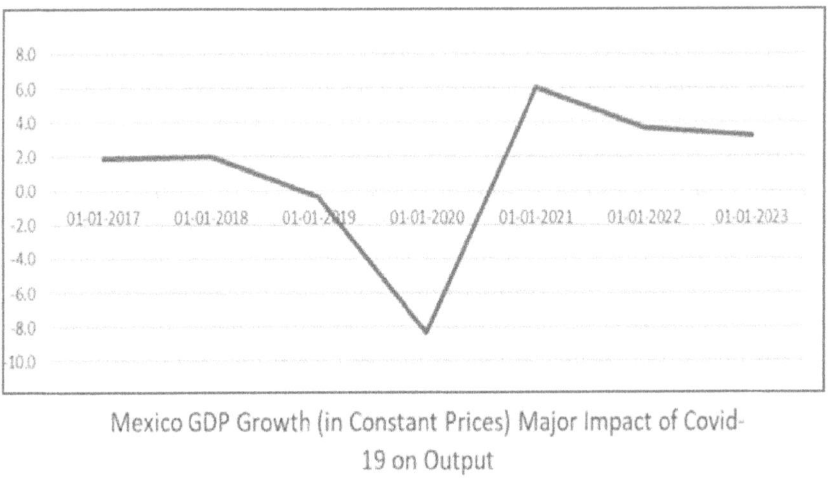

Figure 37: Depicting how the Mexican economy fared during the pandemic period. *Sourced from Macrobond Data. Chart: Karan Mehrishi.*

While she did not initially think of this career, and intended to be a criminal lawyer, central banking soon became her primary interest, and she has spent over five years understanding the nuances of laws governing banking and commercial enterprises, honing her skills fervently.

Aitana did have plans for public service initially, as she intended to join mainstream politics at a later stage of her life; precisely why she chose to study Law and Politics at university. She, however, soon realized that this wasn't her calling, and her contributions to society would rather come from her work within an institutional setting, and administration.

She remembers that her parents encouraged her to choose whatever made her happy. After joining ITAM for a bachelor's coursework, Aitana started her internship in the final two years of her degree and finally joined a public institution as a lawyer.

Despite dropping the idea of starting as a full-fledged politician, Aitana continues to carry her values in whatever she does as a professional, a policymaker, and on a personal level. She says that,

'I am very passionate about equal rights for all'.

Aitana, therefore, takes her social justice streak seriously and supports feminist movements that stand for providing equal rights to women across the world.

A strong personality, Aitana commits to causes that matter in the grander scheme of things, and those which she thinks are critical for human evolution and justice. This trait, she carries in her professional role, as well as in her function as a public administrator.

At a very early stage in her career, Aitana got the opportunity to plan and manage a policy initiative that proved extremely productive during the COVID-19 era in helping vulnerable households, as well as small businesses. She says that this initiative is known today as 'her baby'.

The success of this policy enterprise gave Aitana a lot of confidence in her chosen career and has prepared her to take on bigger responsibilities in her profession.

Dealing with the COVID-19 pandemic, Aitana not only focused on her own well-being but also ensured others were aware and safe. She says that going to the office twice or thrice a week was never a problem during the pandemic, 'because it was part of my job, as a public services professional'.

On a scale of 1–10 (10 being highest), when asked about how frightened she was while performing her duties during the pandemic, Aitana quickly replies with '2 or 3', confidently. She thanks her immunity for this natural resilience.

When asked about her journey so far and her commitment to her nation, Aitana says,

'I became aware of my nationality at the age of 9, when I travelled to Germany. Since then, I have always believed that I will play an important role in my country's development, as a public servant'.

Thanking her sister as a great inspiration and the 'air beneath her wings', Aitana intends to continuously forge ahead on her chosen path in public services.

Travelling to Africa, the story of Victoria Manuel from Namibia is that of struggles, and back-breaking journey of hard work to break the shackles of social isolation and despair. While Victoria is today a monetary economist, and as part of the MPC secretariat between 2017 and 2022, she organized the Namibian Central Bank's first MPC in the COVID-19 era, her journey is a case study of what makes an erudite and effective administrator during a crisis.

As a single mother, Victoria carried her newborn baby while conducting a critical MPC meeting virtually, during the crisis, when the central bank had cut 100 bps, a significant monetary move to fight the COVID-19-related insecurities. In fact, COVID-19-related lockdowns and border closures with the rest of the world were the first time Victoria deeply thought about her nationality, as a Namibian.

This thought filled her with more courage and determination to serve her nation during the difficult times.

When asked about her resilience and grit, Victoria says that she walked about 10 km every day just to get to school, and the same journey back home in the afternoon. As a child studying in primary and secondary school, she left home at 4:30 am with other children, just to reach school on time.

'If I could do that, I could do anything', she said.

While attending university, in Windhoek, the capital city of Namibia, Victoria, and her sister struggled to make money for food and survived by braiding people's hair as undergraduate students.

The struggles paid off, and Victoria graduated with a Bachelor's degree in Economics from the biggest university in Namibia, the University of Namibia, and soon joined a commercial bank as an intern. From here, she soon moved

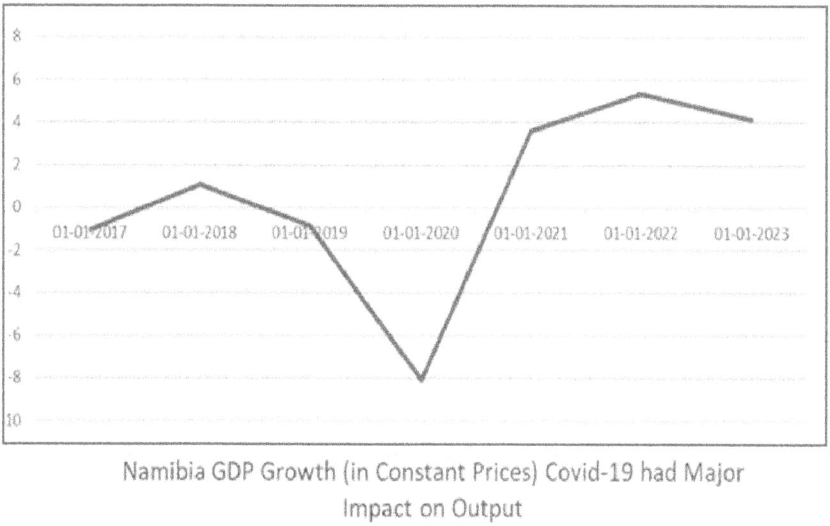

Figure 38: Depicting how the Namibian economy fared during the pandemic period. *Sourced from Macrobond Data. Chart: Karan Mehrishi.*

to Namibia's National Planning Commission, as an economist – performing, research, and forecasting functions for the Namibian national economy.

As fate would have it, Victoria's interactions with the representatives of the Namibian Central Bank later convinced her of becoming a monetary economist, and she decided to apply for a role. Her acceptance into the position made her realize the important role she was playing in public policy and in sustaining the evolving Namibian economy.

Victoria says that her nation has come far over the years, and the current generation does not go through the same kind of struggles that she once faced. Nevertheless, she is thankful for the opportunities she has now, and is proud of her achievements when looking back at her journey. When asked about what went through her mind when COVID-19 struck, she replies calmly, 'there is nothing to be scared of, when doing the work that has been entrusted to you'.

The central bank, she says, not only reduced interest rates but also sustained households and businesses by providing various COVID-19 relief measures such as loan repayment moratoriums, liquidity relief, and relaxation of some prudential measures, among other accommodations.

Victoria says that in most parts of Africa, people follow the 'Ubuntu' philosophy, which simply translates to, 'I am, because we are'. This selfless, family-oriented lifestyle already made Victoria aware of her responsibilities as a young woman growing professionally and personally. Public service is therefore just an extension of her personality, she quips.

The next story involves Yuta Nakazato, a bureaucrat working in the Japanese Ministry of Finance. Yuta comes from a typical Japanese middle-class family, originally from the city of Sapporo, Hokkaido. While his life experience, unlike others in this chapter, is distinct, given the fact that Japan is an advanced economy, Yuta's own journey is not. He says that 'I am the first person in my family, who works with the Government'. Yuta broke the shackles of social isolation by attending the elite University of Tokyo and is a qualified lawyer. 'Typical path for Tokyo Law graduates is Government administration, or mainstream bureaucracy', he says, and that was his path all along.

But there was a bigger story behind Yuta's move into public service, and it started much before he entered Tokyo University. In his formative years, China began to make inroads into Japan's exclusive economic zones, agitating the Japanese public. North Korea, another neighbour, also began to test Japanese patience by firing missiles into the Sea of Japan.

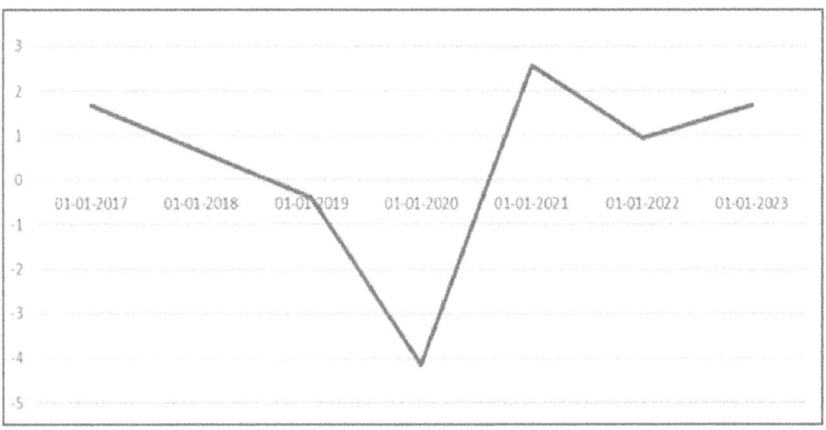

Japan GDP Growth (in Constant Prices) Significant Impact of Covid-19 on Output

Figure 39: Depicting how the Japanese economy fared during the pandemic period.

Sourced from Macrobond Data. Chart: Karan Mehrishi.

This significantly influenced a young Yuta's psychology, and he took up English debating while at school. This inclination allowed Yuta to travel to several countries, representing Japan, at world debating forums. It was here that he says he got a taste of diplomacy, and 'began to see the meritocracy of people from other countries. The fact that all humans are fundamentally the same, was a revelation', he says.

Post his studies, Yuta decided to join the Ministry of Finance, and rose in the ranks, because of his quick learnings and global perspectives, invaluable for public service, at the national level. When the COVID-19 crisis hit Japan, Yuta was at the frontier of policy making, and was on the team that deliberated and designed the cash transfer scheme for households. The scheme that was worth more than 2 per cent of the Japanese GDP, or around 10 per cent of the total Japanese national budget during the year, was revolutionary and provided an equivalent of ~$700 per person as cash support during the crisis.

Yuta says that he was of the opinion that the economy must be quickly normalized as soon as possible, and that the cash transfer scheme was one way of doing that. Even though, the scheme was a one-off, the idea was well-received, and several schemes focusing on the underprivileged and vulnerable households continued throughout the crisis.

Yuta's experience as a policymaker, and the resolve to solve the problems at hand, weren't taken sitting in an ivory tower; instead, they also emanated from his personal life. He says that his mother lost her job during the crisis that ensued with COVID, because retailers were under stress, and 'with-contact' work suffered because people no longer felt comfortable going to public places due to the fear of catching the infection.

The fact that COVID-19 spread quickly in Sapporo, Yuta's home town, ravaging its local economy, was perhaps the other important consideration, influencing his decisions and recommendations as a bureaucrat. Even though infection rates in Japan were never alarming and always under control, there was a risk of proliferation, and insecurities about the ultimate length of the crisis remained daunting for policymakers. Nevertheless, Japan's well-developed medical infrastructure, as well as solid corporate culture ensured health, as well as financial stability, and policy support from the fiscal and monetary sides continued unabated throughout the crises.

An almost ZIRP, as well as guaranteed loans to the corporate sector (especially MSMEs), was a great support system in place, and ensured a robust public confidence, says Yuta. When asked about the fear he faced (both in terms of health risk, as well as responsibility) while performing his duties as a public official on a scale of 1–10 (10 being the highest), Yuta responds with, '3 or 4'. He says that he was always secure and knew about the importance of his service for the public good. Perhaps a thought process which most other public servants across the world shared, allowing humanity to deal with one of its most crippling and daunting crises ever, in over a century.

Based on all the interactions presented above, this author is convinced that no event, irrespective of its magnitude, can ever win against human fortitude and tenacity to live, and thrive. To an extent, these perspectives give a ray of hope, or a sense that, come what may, humanity will always find a way to survive, as a collective. Thankfully, those who lead are always the product of unique life experiences, and these young professionals seem to have always operated with this very understanding. Macroeconomic analysis is for a later day.

Disclaimer: The views presented in this chapter are personal and those of the professionals interviewed and are not representative of their institutions or affiliations.

CHAPTER 11

Conclusion

The management of the COVID-19 pandemic since March 2020 has been the most significant macroeconomic exercise ever undertaken by the Indian Government and the RBI. The situation was akin to the macroeconomic management done during India's 1965, 1971, and 1999 wars with Pakistan and the 1962 war with China – only that this emergency operation lasted for almost three years.

All this brought about the introduction of stimulus packages (five in total so far) worth around ₹26.2 lac crore, which is roughly equal to 9.6 per cent of India's FY23 GDP of ₹273 lac crore. Adding this sum to the monetary stimulus of roughly ₹18.86 lac crore that was provided by the RBI, the total stimulus provided by India to its economy came to be around ₹45.06 lac crore, or 16.5 per cent of the current Indian GDP (FY23).

After contracting for two straight quarters, and ultimately contracting by (−) 6.8 per cent in FY21, the Indian economy has since recovered and regained lost ground rather quickly.

However, as both the domestic and international economic environment did not fully normalize and inflation (along with accompanying rising interest rates) and a significant public debt overhang still haunt policymakers going forward.

As India confidently moves towards becoming a $5 trillion economy by FY27–28, there are lessons to be drawn from India's COVID macroeconomic response. Imbibing these learnings will hold India in good stead if faced with a similar situation in the future. The research in the preceding pages is therefore an attempt to consolidate the macroeconomic response concisely and systematically for macroeconomists, and research scholars, who can utilize this material for their work in the field.

CHAPTER 12

Literature Review of Significant Work Done on the Subject

Literature Review: A Brief Discussion of Important Works on the Subject

A significant level of research on the global macroeconomic response to the pandemic was done by the World Bank Group economists, and several papers and articles are available across the media.

The most significant among these publications was the 'World Development Report 2022: Finance for an equitable recovery'.[145]

Divided into six chapters, the report comprehensively discusses the strategies employed by governments across the world, and this includes fiscal responses, safeguarding households, liquidity provisions to businesses, and providing stable bank balance sheets (based on managing non-performing loan accounts management).

The World Bank report also acknowledges limitations of Government interventions, given the fact that there is a possibility of an ever-increasing public debt to GDP ratio, which in some cases (for poorer countries) may become unsustainable.

Rising levels of inequality, due to considerable job losses, as well as lack of formal financing, and rising household financial vulnerabilities are relevant topics, the report covers in detail.

The later chapters also discuss bad loan management, via timely regulations, dispute resolution, bankruptcy, and asset reconstruction, in detail.

145 https://www.worldbank.org/en/publication/wdr2022/brief/chapter-1-introduction-the-economic-impacts-of-the-covid-19-crisis

Renowned economist, Carmen M. Reinhart, in her paper, 'From Health Crises to Financial Distress' (World Bank: Policy Research Working Paper),[146] provides an insightful analysis of the real per capita GDP losses during crisis periods, and the fact that COVID-19 pandemic era saw the maximum declines.

Following this analysis, Reinhart introduces us to the multiple varieties of financial crises, as well as the historical evolution/stages of banking/sovereign debt crises.

Reinhart notes that emerging and developing economies have limited fiscal and monetary capacities to respond (as compared to developed/advanced economies) when lockdowns and economic hardships are imposed upon national economies due to events such as the COVID-19 pandemic.

By astutely using the old adage, 'this time it's different', Reinhart narrates the story of financial bubbles, which are created during fiscal and monetary accommodations. This invariably turns into a full-blown financial crisis that is hard to contain by concerned Governments.

In their groundbreaking research paper, 'The Macroeconomic effects of Covid-19 on Montenegro: A Bayesian VaRX Approach',[147] economists, Djurovic, Bojaj et al., assess the Output Gap (HP Filtered) using a Litterman/Minnesota prior (Bayesian VaRX).

The independent variables here range from unemployment, tourism, health expenditure, and capital stock. Hypothetical sensitivity scenarios were also introduced in their model, with scenarios spanning ±10 per cent and ±60 per cent. Under various scenarios, economic impacts were assessed, and policy measures were recommended by the authors.

Guy Carpenter's 'An Update from: The Covid-19 Task Force',[148] published on March 24th 2020, provided a comprehensive overview of the initial impact of the pandemic on the global economy.

146 'From Health Crises to Financial Distress' (World Bank: Policy Research Working Paper)

147 https://jfin-swufe.springeropen.com/articles/10.1186/s40854-020-00207-z

148 https://www.marshmclennan.com/content/dam/mmc-web/insights/publications/2020/april/April%20Insurer%20Article%202020%20March%20Covid%20Macroeconomic.pdf

The paper suggested that a decline in the range of 30–35 per cent was recorded by important equity markets across the world as the pandemic started to spread in the initial months of 2020. The only precedents, according to the authors, were in '1987, 2001, and 2008'.

A detailed assessment further discusses the impact on the outlook set by rating agencies, and how their earlier actions will have to be modified given the new ground realities.

Another notable work on the impact of COVID-19 on the Indian economy is 'How has Covid-19 affected India's economy? (Economics Observatory),'[149] authored by LSE economists, Swati Dhingra, and Maitreesh Ghatak.

The authors delve into micro-level data and try to decipher the impact on the ground. Referring to the work of Pew Research (Rakesh Kochhar),[150] the authors state that due to the pandemic, 'the number of poor are projected to have doubled, and the middle class has fallen'.

Referring to the works of Azim Premji University's Centre for Sustainable Employment,[151] the authors also suggest that incomes declined by 40 per cent between April and May 2020 – the initial months of the COVID-19 lead lockdowns.

Furthermore, by using the data from CMIE Consumer Pyramid's Households Survey[152] (CPHS), the authors manage to prove that the pandemic had far-reaching effects on the Indian macroeconomy, and households were under significant duress during and after the lockdown periods.

According to the CMIE CPHS data, 'per capita consumption spending was 20 per cent lower in August 2020 (YoY), and 15 per cent lower towards the end of that year'. The CPHS data also showcases that rural and urban poverty levels in India increased by over 14 per cent and 18 per cent, respectively, during 2020.

149 https://www.economicsobservatory.com/how-has-covid-19-affected-indias-economy

150 https://www.pewresearch.org/short-reads/2021/03/18/in-the-pandemic-indias-middle-class-shrinks-and-poverty-spreads-while-china-sees-smaller-changes/

151 https://azimpremjiuniversity.edu.in/cse

152 https://consumerpyramidsdx.cmie.com/

Not difficult to fathom, with the help of official government (MOSPI) data, the authors also point to the almost doubling of unemployment levels during the period.

In yet another comprehensive research, economists Zamfir and Lordhach et al. provide a robust methodology to assess the impact on the economy due to pandemic-related measures during the pandemic.

The authors utilize the Principal Components Analysis (PCA) approach as their primary tool in this assessment to compare various European countries as a system.

In their paper, 'The Influences of Covid-19 Pandemic on Macroeconomic Indexes for European Countries' (Taylor & Francis: Applied Economics),[153] the authors identify the primary components as wages, final household consumption expenditure, Government debt, labour productivity, subsidies, and trade, among others.

In their paper, 'What Works to Control Covid-19?[154] Econometric Analysis of a Cross-Country Panel', Asian Development Bank (ADB) economists, Chen, Raitzer, Hasan, et al., use empirical regression model (cross-country regression framework, comprising of 70 countries) to assess the impact of Non-Pharmaceutical Interventions (NPI), on COVID-19 transmission rates, as well as economic activity (GDP).

In order to prepare a comprehensive list of NPI, the authors include variables such as 'extent of testing', 'bans', 'use of masks', 'tracing, and isolation', among others.

What makes this research stand out is the use of 'country-specific features', which may affect control measure efficacy, as well as the use of Paid-Sick Leaves (PSL) as a control measure in the analysis.

As one of the earliest attempts to assess the macroeconomic impact of the COVID-19 pandemic, the paper, 'Forecast of China's Economic Growth during the Covid-19 Pandemic:[155]

A MIDAS Regression Analysis (Emerald Insight)', economists Gunay, Can, Ocak et al., is an insightful read.

153 https://www.tandfonline.com/doi/full/10.1080/00036846.2022.2031858

154 https://papers.ssrn.com/sol3/papers.cfm?abstract_id=3785083

155 https://www.emerald.com/insight/content/doi/10.1108/JCEFTS-08-2020-0053/full/html

The authors utilize a Mixed Data Sampling regression, along with Markov-Switching, and OLS methodologies in their empirical analysis of high-frequency data (ranging from daily, monthly, and quarterly).

Perhaps the most significant finding of this research was that the dummy variables that were used for the GFC are found to be insignificant in the assessment of COVID-19.

This points to the fact that COVID-19's macroeconomic drivers had a different mechanism compared to the GFC macroeconomic impact on any given economy.

Another important research comes from economists, Keogh-Brown, Jensen, et al., who attempt to model the direct and indirect impact of the pandemic on the UK economy. In their paper, 'The Impact of Covid-19, Associated Behaviours, and Policies, on the UK Economy:[156]

A Computational General Equilibrium Model (Elsevier)', the authors use a CGE model linked to an Epidemiological model to ascertain the impact (and associated costs of managing) the pandemic.

Given the paper's publication in December 2020, the assessment is initial, and as per the findings of the authors, the health-related economic burden on the UK economy was estimated to be 1.73 per cent (of UK GDP).

Mitigation strategies (in terms of school and business closures), according to the authors, however, had cost the UK economy a GDP worth 13.5 per cent. Long-term mitigation strategies, the authors believed, would have cost the UK economy a significant 29.2 per cent of GDP.

A research paper, 'Macroeconomic Impact of Covid-19: Post Covid Era:[157] Future of Economics & World Order (Istanbul University Press)', written by economists, Cak, Goksel, and Bozoklu, also provides a rigorous understanding via the construction of a Dynamic General Equilibrium Model (DSGE), representing the Government side (Fiscal), Business side (Firm), and the Household side.

The purpose of the modelling was to determine the pandemic-driven shocks on the GDP, and its major components (primarily from the Aggregate Demand perspective).

156 https://www.sciencedirect.com/science/article/pii/S2352827320302883

157 https://iupress.istanbul.edu.tr/en/book/post-covid-era-future-of-economies-and-world-order/chapter/macroeconomic-impacts-of-covid-19

Through their analysis, the authors try to ascertain the most robust fiscal response to the pandemic, and suggest that 'Government subsidized consumption in the short term', is perhaps the most effective tool for optimal welfare stability. The authors' research does not support longer-term Government subsidy (in this context), as that is subject to a crowding-out effect.

In groundbreaking research, economists, Raj Chetty, John N Freidman, et al., in their paper, 'The Economic Impact of Covid-19: Evidence from a New Public Dataset built using Private Sector Data[158] (Oxford Academics: The Quarterly Journal of Economics)', show that public data (job-postings, company-revenues, employment-rates, and consumer-spending) accessed from the private sector can shed significant light on the impact on the economy due to the pandemic related shocks.

Dissecting the data at the 'granular level', the authors successfully show how the pandemic-related shocks impacted different 'sub-groups'.

Such granular-level data allows the authors to do real-time data analysis (in terms of marginal consumption propensities), and assist in their conclusion that in the shorter term, incentives (such as cash payments) successfully helped low-income households.

Overall findings of the authors suggest that the fiscal aid is an effective tool to contain the mall-effects of job losses, and household consumption slowdown ('during the initial shock').

NBER working paper, 'Transfers Vs Credit Policy:[159] Macroeconomic Policy Trade-offs during Covid-19', by economists Bigio, Zhang, and Zilberman, is another interesting assessment, where the trade-off between the efficacy of Government transfers (in full) and credit policy (subsidised) is ascertained.

The authors suggest that subsidized transfers are a potent weapon to fight recession in developing countries, whereas the 'unleashing of credit' should be the preferred policy for the developed countries (these assumptions are made with adherence to the Ricardian Equivalence).

158 https://academic.oup.com/qje/article/139/2/829/7289247?login=false
159 https://papers.ssrn.com/sol3/papers.cfm?abstract_id=3597850

A noteworthy contribution of the authors in this paper is that they base their findings (pertaining to household propensities based on the elasticity of substitution assumption) on the equivalence of (and substitution of) 'goods needing social interactions, and goods consumed remotely', defining these two goods collectively, as a 'composite good' equivalent.

In the volume, 'The Covid-19 Pandemic, India and the World:[160] Economic and Social Policy Perspective' (Routledge) edited by Bhattacharyya et al., economist Ajitava Raychaudhuri tries to assess the 'short-run & long-term issues', impacting India during the crisis. Raychaudhuri uses a Keynesian macroeconomic framework, incorporating demand and supply shocks, in combination with the evolution of the balance of payment scenarios. The author contends that in the short term, signals from the fiscal and monetary packages may not be successful in bringing about desired multiplier effects (from the demand side).

At the same time, factor constraints may limit the supply side. In the longer term, the author foresees the importance of foreign inflows into India and the resultant benefits they bring to the macroeconomy.

Finally, while there are several other contributions in the field, it may not be possible to review all due to the constraints of time and space, but this author feels that two noteworthy contributions also deserve references in this 'Literature Review' chapter.

The papers, 'Macroeconomic Policy in the Time of Covid-19:[161] A Primer for Developing Countries (The World Bank Group)', written by economists, Norman Loayza, and Steven Pennings, and 'An Assessment of Unconventional Monetary Policy During Covid-19 Pandemic in India'[162] (SAGE Journals), written by economists D. Tripati Rao, and Rahul Kumar, are honourable mentions in this section.

160 https://www.routledge.com/The-COVID-19-Pandemic-India-and-the-World-Economic-and-Social-Policy-Perspectives/Bhattacharyya-GhoshDastidar-Sikdar/p/book/9781032114965

161 https://papers.ssrn.com/sol3/papers.cfm?abstract_id=3586636

162 https://journals.sagepub.com/doi/abs/10.1177/09726527231163207

Bibliography

Adrian, Tobias and Boyarchenko, Nina. "Liquidity Policy and Systemic Risk". Federal Reserve Bank of New York Staff Reports, no. 661. December 2013. <https://www.newyorkfed.org/medialibrary/media/research/staff_reports/sr661.pdf>

Annual Report Publications Data. *Reserve Bank of India*. 2024. <https://www.rbi.org.in/Scripts/AnnualReportPublications.aspx?year=2024>

Association of Mutual Funds in India (AMFI) data: <https://www.amfiindia.com/indian-mutual>

Azim Premji University Website. <https://azimpremjiuniversity.edu.in/cse>

"Banking System to be Flushed with Liquidity as CRR cut to 3 per cent". *The Hindu Business Line*. 27 March 2020. <https://www.thehindubusinessline.com/money-and-banking/banking-system-will-be-flush-with-liquidity-as-crr-cut-to-3-per-cent/article31178978.ece>

Barik, S. S. "Basel III Framework on Liquidity Standards – Liquidity Coverage Ratio (LCR), Liquidity Risk Monitoring Tools and LCR Disclosure Standard". *RBI*, 2 Aug 2017. <https://www.rbi.org.in/commonman/english/Scripts/Notification.aspx?Id=2490>

Behera, Harenda Kumar. "Updating Estimates of the Natural Rate of Interest for India with Post-Pandemic Evidence". *RBI Monthly Bulletin*, vol. 78, no. 7 July 2024. <https://rbidocs.rbi.org.in/rdocs/Bulletin/PDFs/0BULLETINJULY18072024C1D39FE2E7AB4F8893C8E207C7818398.PDF>

Bernanke, Ben S. "Governor Speech on the Global Savings Glut and the US Current Account Deficit". *EliScholar*, 10 March 2005. <https://elischolar.library.yale.edu/cgi/viewcontent.cgi?article=5269&context=ypfs-documents>

Bernstein et al. "Identifying the Effects of a Lender of Last Resort on Financial Markets: Lessons from the Founding of the Fed". *Journal of Financial Economics* 98, 2010, pp. 40–53. *ScienceDirect*. <https://leeds-faculty.colorado.edu/asafbernstein/Bernstein_Hughson_Weidenmier_FoundingOfFed.pdf>

Bhat, Swati and Dugal, Ira. "Real Rate of About 1% Appropriate For Indian Economy: Rate Panel's Goyal". *Reuters*, 23 February 2023. <https://www.reuters.com/world/india/real-interest-rate-about-1-appropriate-indian-economy-rate-panels-goyal-2023-02-23/>

Bhat, Swati and Nayak, Siddhi. "Neutral Rate Cannot Determine Monetary Policy in India, Says Cen Bank Chief". *Reuters*, 19 July 2024. <https://www.reuters.com/world/india/neutral-rate-cannot-determine-monetary-policy-india-says-cenbank-

chief-2024-07-19/#:~:text=The%20central%20bank%20in%20its,referring%20to%20the%20latest%20study>.

Bhattacharyya et al. "The COVID-19 Pandemic, India and the WorldEconomic and Social Policy Perspectives". *Routledge India*, 30 September 2021. <https://www.routledge.com/The-COVID-19-Pandemic-India-and-the-World-Economic-and-Social-Policy-Perspectives/Bhattacharyya-GhoshDastidar-Sikdar/p/book/9781032114965>

Bigio et al. "Transfers vs Credit Policy: Macroeconomic Policy Trade-Offs During Covid-19". NBER Working Paper No. w27118, 12 May 2020. *NBER*. <https://papers.ssrn.com/sol3/papers.cfm?abstract_id=3597850>

BIS India Institutional Framework. *BIS*. <https://www.bis.org/mc/currency_areas/in.htm>

Boragan Auroba, S. and Diebold, Francis X. "Real-Time Measurement of Business Conditions". *Journal of Business and Economic Statistics*, Sep 2008. *ResearchGate*. <https://www.researchgate.net/publication/228272358_Real-Time_Measurement_of_Business_Conditions>

"Cabinet Approves Covid Stimulus Package for ₹ 6.29 lac crores". *The Economic Times*. 30 June 2021. <https://economictimes.indiatimes.com/news/economy/policy/cabinet-approves-rs-6-29-lakh-crore-covid-19-relief-package-announced-by-fm/articleshow/83985109.cms?from=mdr>

Camacho et al. "Dynamic Factor Markov-Switching Models in Real Time". International Journal of Forecasting, vol. 34, no. 4, pp. 598–611, October–December 2018. *ScienceDirect*. <https://www.sciencedirect.com/science/article/abs/pii/S0169207018300773>

Carlson et al. "The Effects of Banking Competition on Growth and Financial Stability: Evidence from the National Banking Era". *Journal of Political Economy*, vol. 130, no. 2, February 2022. *University of Chicago University Press Journals*. <https://www.journals.uchicago.edu/doi/10.1086/717453>

Carlson, Mark A. and Wheelock, David C. "The Lender of Last Resort: Lessons from the Fed's First 100 Years". *FRB of St. Louis Working Paper No. 2012-056B*. Federal Reserve Bank of St. Luis, 2012. <https://papers.ssrn.com/sol3/papers.cfm?abstract_id=2173391>

Carlson, Mark. "The Young Fed: The Banking Crises of the 1920s and the Making of a Lender of Last Resort". University of Chicago Press, 2025. <https://press.uchicago.edu/ucp/books/book/chicago/Y/bo239243080.html>

Chattopadhyay, S.K., Mitra, A.K. "Monetary policy transmission in India under the base rate and MCLR regimes: a comparative study". *Humanities and Social Sciences Communications* 10, 2023. <https://doi.org/10.1057/s41599-023-01883-9>

Charmal, Vikas and Goyal, Ashima. "Liquidity Management and Monetary Transmission: Empirical Analysis for India". Journal of Economic Studies, 4 July 2022; 49 (5):

850–875. *Emerald Insight*. <https://www.emerald.com/insight/content/doi/10.1108/jes-07-2020-0359/full/html>

Chen et al. "What Works to Control COVID-19? Econometric Analysis of a Cross-Country Panel?". Asian Development Bank Economics Working Paper Series, No. 625, 16 February 2021. *SSRN*. <https://papers.ssrn.com/sol3/papers.cfm?abstract_id=3785083>

Chetty et al. "The Economic Impacts of COVID-19: Evidence from a New Public Database Built Using Private Sector Data". *The Quarterly Journal of Economics*, vol. 139, Issue 2, May 2024, pp. 829–889. Oxford Academic. <https://academic.oup.com/qje/article/139/2/829/7289247?login=false>

Chugh et al. "India's growing capital market: Promising first steps to internationalization". *S&P Global*, 19 September 2024. <https://www.spglobal.com/en/research-insights/special-reports/india-forward/indias-growing-capital-market-promising-first-steps-to-internationalization>

Consumer Pyramids dx website. <https://consumerpyramidsdx.cmie.com/>

Coronavirus cases in India. *Worldometer*. <https://www.worldometers.info/coronavirus/country/india/>

Covid Death Toll Statistics (India Page). *Google*. <https://news.google.com/covid19/map?hl=en-IN&mid=%2Fm%2F03rk0&gl=IN&ceid=IN%3Aen>

CRISIL Ratings: Default Ratings Transitions Study, up to Fiscal 2022. *CRISILRatings*. <https://www.crisilratings.com/content/dam/crisil/our-analysis/publications/default-study/crisil-ratings-annual-default-and-ratings-transition-study-fy-2022.pdf>

Çak et al. "Macroeconomic Impacts of Covid-19". *Post Covid Era: Future of Economies and World Order. An Interdisciplinary Approach*, ed. Baykal et al. Istanbul University Press. *Istanbul University Press*. <https://iupress.istanbul.edu.tr/en/book/post-covid-era-future-of-economies-and-world-order/chapter/macroeconomic-impacts-of-covid-19>

Das, Shaktikanta. Governor's Statement. *RBI*, 8 April 2022. <https://www.rbi.org.in/commonman/english/scripts/PressReleases.aspx?Id=3352>

Dayal, Yogesh. RBI Monetary Policy Meeting Summary. *Reserve Bank of India*, 20 April 2020. <https://www.rbi.org.in/Scripts/BS_PressReleaseDisplay.aspx?prid=49700>

Debortoli et al. "IMF Working Paper: Designing a Simple Loss Function for Central Banks". IMF Working Papers, vol. 17, no. 164.

Del Negro et al. "Safety, Liquidity, and Natural Rate of Interest". *Federal Reserve Bank of New York*, no. 812, May 2017. <https://www.newyorkfed.org/research/staff_reports/sr812.html>

de Valk et al. "Nowcasting: An R Package for Predicting Economic Variables Using DFM". The R Journal, vol 11/01, Jun 2019. <https://journal.r-project.org/archive/2019/RJ-2019-020/RJ-2019-020.pdf>

Diaz, Elena Maria and Perez-Quiroz, Gabriel. "GEA Tracker: A Daily Indicator of Global Economic Activity". *Journal of International Money and Finance*, vol. 115, July 2021. *ScienceDirect*. <https://www.sciencedirect.com/science/article/abs/pii/S0261560621000498>

Diamond, William and Van Tassel, Peter. "A Look at Convenience Yields Across the World". *Liberty Street Economics*, 3 October 2023. <https://libertystreeteconomics.newyorkfed.org/2023/10/a-look-at-convenience-yields-around-the-world/>

Djurovic et al. "The macroeconomic effects of COVID-19 in Montenegro: a Bayesian VARX approach". *Financial Innovation*, vol. 6, 10 November 2020. *SpringerOpen*. <https://jfin-swufe.springeropen.com/articles/10.1186/s40854-020-00207-z>

Dhingra, Swati and Ghatak, Maithreesh. "How Has Covid-19 Affected Indian Economy?". *EconomicsObservatory*, 30 June 2021. <https://www.economicsobservatory.com/how-has-covid-19-affected-indias-economy>

Dooley, Michael. "Can emerging economy central banks be market makers of last resort?". *BIS*. <https://www.bis.org/publ/bppdf/bispap79k.pdf>

Eichengreen et al. "India's Debt Dilemma". India Policy Forum, 6–7 July 2023. *NCAER*, <https://www.ncaer.org/wp-content/uploads/2023/07/Paper-I-Barry-Poonam.pdf>

Eichengreen et al. "Inflation Targeting in India: An Interim Assessment". *World Bank Group*, 2021. <https://openknowledge.worldbank.org/server/api/core/bitstreams/bfd1f553-0baf-5e3e-8644-86ae90be697b/content>

Forward Looking Survey: SPF Forecasts Round 93. *RBI*, 9 April 2025. <https://www.rbi.org.in/Scripts/PublicationsView.aspx?id=23144>

FRED Data on US Output Gap. *Federal Reserve Bank of St.Louis*. <https://fred.stlouisfed.org/graph/?g=f1cZ>

Fischer, Stanley. "The Lender of Last Resort Function in the United States". *Federal Reserve Board*, 2016. <https://www.federalreserve.gov/newsevents/speech/fischer20160210a.htm>

"From Health Crises to Financial Distress". *World Bank*, Policy Research Working Paper. <https://www.worldbank.org/en/publication/wdr2022/brief/chapter-1-introduction-the-economic-impacts-of-the-covid-19-crisis>

Fuster et al. "Mortgage-Backed Securities (MBS)" Staff Report no. 1001, February 2022. *Federal Reserve Bank of New York*. <https://www.newyorkfed.org/medialibrary/media/research/staff_reports/sr1001.pdf>

Giannone et al. "Nowcasting: The Real-Time Informational Content of Macroeconomic Data". *Journal of Monetary Economics*, vol. 55, no. 4, pp. 665–676, May 2008. *Elsevier*. <https://www.sciencedirect.com/science/article/pii/S0304393208000652>

Gilchrist, Simon and Zakrajsek, Egon. "NBER Working Paper: INVESTMENT AND THE COST OF CAPITAL: NEW EVIDENCE FROM THE CORPORATE

BOND MARKET". *NBER Working Paper Series*, 2007. <https://www.nber.org/system/files/working_papers/w13174/w13174.pdf>

Government of India, Ministry of Finance. India Budget Statistics. <https://www.indiabudget.gov.in/>

Government of India, Ministry of Finance, Press Bureau. "Finance Minister announces Rs 1.70 Lakh Crore relief package under Pradhan Mantri Garib Kalyan Yojana for the poor to help them fight the battle against Corona Virus". *PIB*. 26 March 2020. <https://pib.gov.in/PressReleaseIframePage.aspx?PRID=1608345>

Government of India, Ministry of Finance, Press Bureau. "Atmannirbhar Bharat Package Announcement". *PIB*. 12 November 2020. <https://static.pib.gov.in/WriteReadData/userfiles/Atmanirbhar%20Package%203.0%20final%20final%20%20-%20Copy%201.pdf>

Gunay et al. "Forecast of China's economic growth during the COVID-19 pandemic: a MIDAS regression analysis". *Journal of Chinese Economic and Foreign Trade Studies*, vol. 14, pp. 3–17, 30 December 2020. *EmeraldInsight*. <https://www.emerald.com/insight/content/doi/10.1108/JCEFTS-08-2020-0053/full/html>

Households Inflation Expectations Survey. *RBI*, 9 April 2025. <https://www.rbi.org.in/Scripts/PublicationsView.aspx?id=23147>

"How Money Markets Fared in H1FY24?". *Aditya Birla Capital Mutual Fund*, 2023. <https://mutualfund.adityabirlacapital.com/abslamc-knowledge-centre/articles/how-have-money-markets-fared-in-h1fy24>

India CPI Data. *Ministry of Statistics and Program Implementation Press Releases*. <https://www.mospi.gov.in/web/mospi/press-release1>

India FDI Policy. *Invest India*. <https://www.investindia.gov.in/foreign-direct-investment>

India GDP Annual Growth Rate. *Trading Economics*. <https://tradingeconomics.com/india/gdp-growth-annual>

Kalsie, Anjala and Yadav, Ashutosh. "Drivers of WACR-Repo Rate Spread: An Empirical Analysis of India". *SageJournals*, 2023. <https://doi.org/10.1177/09721509231166257>

Kant et al. "Nowcasting GDP Using Machine Learning Methods". *DNB*, working paper no. 754, November 2022. <https://www.dnb.nl/media/kq4pe4cr/working_paper_no_754.pdf>

Keister, Todd. "Corridors and Floors of Monetary Policy". *Liberty Street Economics*, 2012. <https://libertystreeteconomics.newyorkfed.org/2012/04/corridors-and-floors-in-monetary-policy/>

Kelly, Steven. "How the FDIC sourced crisis time Fed funding through the failed banks of 2023". *Yale Program on Financial Stability*, 20 Aug 2024. <https://som.yale.edu/story/2024/how-fdic-sourced-crisis-time-fed-funding-through-failed-banks-2023>

Keogh-Brown et al. "The impact of Covid-19, associated behaviours and policies on the UK economy: A computable general equilibrium model". *SSM – Population Health*, vol. 12, December 2020. *ScienceDirect*. <https://www.sciencedirect.com/science/article/pii/S2352827320302883>

Kochhar, Rakesh. "In the pandemic, India's middle class shrinks and poverty spreads while China sees smaller changes". *Pew Research Center*, 18 March 2021. <https://www.pewresearch.org/short-reads/2021/03/18/in-the-pandemic-indias-middle-class-shrinks-and-poverty-spreads-while-china-sees-smaller-changes/>

Krishnamurthy, Arvind and Vissing-Jorgensen, Annette. "The Aggregate Demand for Treasury Debt". *Journal of Political Economy*, vol. 120, no. 2, April 2012. *University of Chicago Press Journals*. <https://www.journals.uchicago.edu/doi/abs/10.1086/666526>

Kumari, Anjali. "Business Standard: RBI decides to include corporate debt under HTM". *Business Standard*, 13 September 2023. <https://www.business-standard.com/economy/news/rbi-decides-to-include-corporate-bond-under-held-to-maturity-category-123091301131_1.html>

"Liquidity Easing to Moderate Indian Banks' NIMs Pressure as Rates Fall". *FitchRatings*, 2025. <https://www.fitchratings.com/research/banks/liquidity-easing-to-moderate-indian-banks-nim-pressure-as-rates-fall-12-02-2025#:~:text=System%20liquidity%20pressures%20have%20moderated,a%20key%20factor%20to%20watch>.

Mathew, Jiji T. "RBI's Post Covid Monetary and Liquidity Measures: Impact on Money, Bond, and Credit Markets". NIBM Working Paper Series. *NIBM India*. 2022. <https://www.nibmindia.org/static/working_paper/NIBM_WP19_JM.pdf>

Mehrishi, Karan. "How Regulations Have Failed Our Fixed-Income Securities Market". *Mint*, 6 Oct 2021. <https://www.livemint.com/opinion/online-views/how-regulations-have-failed-our-fixed-income-securities-market-11633536507546.html>

Minutes of the Federal Open Market Committee. "Exit Strategy Principals Component". *Federal Reserve Board*. 21–22 June 2011. <https://www.federalreserve.gov/monetarypolicy/fomcminutes20110622.htm>

"Municipal Market: Bonds are acting as bonds again". *Nuveen (TIAA)*. <https://www.nuveen.com/en-us/insights/municipal-bond-investing/municipal-market-bonds-are-acting-like-bonds-again>

Nelson, Bill. "CLF Notes – What is a CLF?". *Bank Policy Institute*, 22 June 2023. <https://bpi.com/wp-content/uploads/2023/06/CLF-Notes-%E2%80%93-What-is-a-Committed-Liquidity-Facility.pdf>

NSDL. India Bond Info. <https://www.indiabondinfo.nsdl.com/>

OBICUS Survey, Q2, 2024–25. *RBI*, 7 February 2025. <https://www.rbi.org.in/Scripts/PublicationsView.aspx?id=23134>

Pancholy, Puneet. Monetary Policy Statement. *RBI*, 9 April 2025. <https://rbi.org.in/Scripts/BS_PressReleaseDisplay.aspx?prid=60176>

Pancholy, Puneet. Monetary Policy Statement. *RBI*, 7 February 2025. <https://www.rbi.org.in/Scripts/BS_PressReleaseDisplay.aspx?prid=59692>

Pancholy, Puneet. Governor's Statement. *RBI*, 7 February 2025. <https://www.rbi.org.in/Scripts/BS_PressReleaseDisplay.aspx?prid=59694>

"Parliament nod sought for extra spend of Rs 3.25 lakh cr on subsidy, capex". *The Economic Times*. 10 December 2022. <https://economictimes.indiatimes.com/news/economy/finance/govt-seeks-parliament-nod-for-net-additional-spending-of-rs-3-25-lakh-cr-this-fiscal/articleshow/96106019.cms>

Pattanaik et al. "Basal III LCR and the Operating Target of Monetary Policy: The Unintended Discord". *Journal of Banking Regulation*, vol. 19, pp. 160–173. *Springer Nature*, 2017. <https://link.springer.com/article/10.1057/s41261-017-0043-2>

Policy Circle Bureau. "Liquidity Crisis Threatens RBI's Economic Growth Push". *Policy Circle*, 2025. <https://www.policycircle.org/economy/liquidity-crisis-threatens-economy/>

PTI. "India Biggest Recipient of FPI Inflows Worth ₹ 2.6 lac crores in FY21". *Deccan Herald*. 31 March 2021. <https://www.deccanherald.com/business/business-news/india-biggest-recipient-of-fpi-inflows-worth-rs-26-lakh-crore-in-fy21-968701.html>

RBI Act. Regulations. *Reserve Bank of India*. <https://m.rbi.org.in/scripts/fs_overview.aspx?fn=2752>

"RBI Surplus Transfer to the Government of India" *Dristi IAS*. 2024. <https://www.drishtiias.com/daily-updates/daily-news-analysis/rbi-surplus-transfer-to-government>

RBI Annual Reports for years 2023–24. *Reserve Bank of India*. <https://rbi.org.in/scripts/AnnualReportPublications.aspx>

RBI Weekly Data for years 2020–2021. *Reserve Bank of India*. <https://rbi.org.in/Scripts/BS_ViewWSS.aspx>

RBI Weekly Data. *RIB*, 7 June 2024. <https://rbi.org.in/Scripts/WSSViewDetail.aspx?TYPE=Basic&PARAM1=6/07/2024>

RBI Weekly Statistical Supplement. *Reserve Bank of India*. <https://rbi.org.in/Scripts/BS_ViewWSS.aspx>

Rees, Daniel and Sun, Guofeng. "The Natural Interest Rate in China". *BIS Working Paper*, no. 949, 9 June 2021. <https://www.bis.org/publ/work949.htm#:~:text=Findings,mirrors%20that%20in%20other%20economies>

"Reliance on Call Money Market Component". Banking Development and Perspectives. *Reserve Bank of India*, 2002. <https://www.rbi.org.in/scripts/PublicationsView.aspx?Id=4555>

"Report of Expert Committee to Revise and Strengthen the Monetary Policy Framework". *Reserve Bank of India*, 2014. <https://rbidocs.rbi.org.in/rdocs/PublicationReport/Pdfs/ECOMRF210114_F.pdf>

Repo Rate Movement. *Bank Bazaar*. <https://www.bankbazaar.com/home-loan/repo-rate.html>

Report on Municipal Finances 2024. *RBI*. <https://m.rbi.org.in/scripts/AnnualPublications.aspx?head=Report%20on%20Municipal%20Finances>

Satya Krishna Sharma, Raavinuthala, Kumar Bijoy, and Arunaditya Sahay. 2022. "Issues in Liquidity Management in Banking System: An Empirical Evidence from Indian Commercial Banks." *Cogent Economics & Finance* 10 (1). doi:10.1080/23322039.2022.2122190.

SIFMA. US Corporate Bond Statistics. <https://www.sifma.org/resources/research/statistics/us-corporate-bonds-statistics/>

Sinha, Saurav. "Basal III Framework on Liquidity Standards" *RBI Notification*, 2020. <https://www.rbi.org.in/commonperson/English/Scripts/Notification.aspx?Id=3237#:~:text=As%20part%20of%20post%20Global,from%20April%201%2C%202020%5D>

Srivastava, Anubha. "Assessing the Dual Facets of Monetary Policy: Profitability and Liquidity in Indian Public and Private Sector Banks". *IndiaStat*, 2024. <https://www.indiastat.com/SOCIO_PDF/Assessing-Dual-Facets-Monetary-Policy-Profitability-Liquidity-Indian-Public-Private-Sector-Banks/Assessing-Dual-Facets-Monetary-Policy-Profitability.pdf>

Statement on Developmental and Regulatory Policies. *RBI*, 2017. <https://www.rbi.org.in/commonman/english/scripts/PressReleases.aspx?Id=2219>

Stock, James H. and Watson, Mark W. "Estimating Turning Points Using Large Data Sets". *Journal of Econometrics*, vol 178, pp. 368–381, January 2014. *Elsevier*. <https://www.sciencedirect.com/science/article/abs/pii/S030440761300198X>

Stock, J. H. and Watson, M. W. "Dynamic Factor Models, Structural Vector Auto Regressions in Macroeconomics". Handbook of Macroeconomics, vol. 2A. Elsevier, 2016. <https://www.princeton.edu/~mwatson/papers/Stock_Watson_HOM_Vol2.pdf>

Subbarao, D. "RBI Monetary Policy Statement". *Reserve Bank of India*, 2011–12. <https://www.voiceofca.in/siteadmin/document/RBI_Monetary_Policy_Statement_for_2011-12_Press_Statement.pdf>

Surti, Jay and Goel, Rohit. "IMF: Corporate Debt Market: Evolution, Prospects, and Policy". *India's Financial System: Building the Foundation for Strong and Sustainable Growth*, ed. Schipke et al., International Monetary Fund, 6 July 2023. *IMF eLibrary*. <https://www.elibrary.imf.org/display/book/9798400223525/CH005.xml>

Survey of Professional Forecasters (SPF). RBI, Round-92nd.

Suvarna, Manish M. "Banks Step up to Borrow through MSF as Liquidity Falls". *Moneycontrol*, 2023. <https://www.moneycontrol.com/news/business/banks-step-up-borrowing-through-msf-as-liquidity-falls-11258981.html>

The Covid-19 Task Force. „Covid-19: a Macroeconomic Perspective". *MarshMcLennan*, 24 March 2020. <https://www.marshmclennan.com/content/dam/mmc-web/insights/publications/2020/april/April%20Insurer%20Article%202020%20March%20Covid%20Macroeconomic.pdf>

"The Manufacturing Sector's Evolution and its Role in an Economy". *Federal Reserve Bank of St. Louis*. 27 March 2018. <https://www.stlouisfed.org/on-the-economy/2018/march/manufacturing-sectors-evolution-role-economy#:~:text=The%20authors%20noted%20that%20this,rapid%20as%20the%20manufacturing%20sector's.%E2%80%9D>

Tripati Rao, D., and Kumar, Rahul. "An Assessment of Unconventional Monetary Policy During COVID-19 Pandemic in India". *SageJournals*, 2023. <https://journals.sagepub.com/doi/abs/10.1177/09726527231163207>

Upasani, Siddharth. "RBI Bulletin: India's Output Gap Now Positive". *Moneycontrol*, 17 August 2023. <https://www.moneycontrol.com/news/business/economy/rbi-bulletin-indias-output-gap-now-positive-stagflation-risk-at-only-3-11211891.html>

US Municipal Bond Statistics. *SIFMA*. <https://www.sifma.org/resources/research/statistics/us-municipal-bonds-statistics/>

Vishwanathan, N. S. "Basal 3 Liquidity Framework - Implementation and Way Forward". *BIS*, 2015. <https://www.bis.org/review/r160111a.pdf>

Zamfir, Ionela-Catalina and Iordache, Ana-Maria Mihaela. "The influences of covid-19 pandemic on macroeconomic indexes for European countries". *Applied Economics*, vol. 54, issue 39, pp. 4519–4531, 2022. *Taylor & Francis Online*.

About the Author

Karan Mehrishi is an Indian economist and financial journalist.

He completed his graduate studies at Yale, Columbia, along with the House of Finance (Hof), Goethe University, Frankfurt, and specializes in monetary economics.

In 2013, Karan Mehrishi was adjudged a *Prize Finalist* for the *IE Business School Prize for Economics Journalism in Asia*.

Previously, he was an economist with a bilateral government agency and a credit rating agency and was trained in equity research at an investment bank in Mumbai.

Karan has so far authored three books on the Indian economy and is also the editor of a book on India's political economy and economic planning.

Index

www.ingramcontent.com/pod-product-compliance
Ingram Content Group UK Ltd.
Pitfield, Milton Keynes, MK11 3LW, UK
UKHW020841290926
15470UKWH00004B/1484

9 781803 747156